Cons

Employment Law for Nurses

John Hodgson

Quay Publishing
BKT Information Services

Quay Publishing Ltd
7.1.9 Cameron House
White Cross, Lancaster LA1 4XQ

ISBN   1-85642-033-7

© **BKT Information Services & Quay Publishing Ltd. 1993**

All rights reserved. No part of this material may be reproduced, stored in a retrieval system, or transmitted in any form, or by any means, electrical, mechanical, photographic, recording, or otherwise, without the prior permission of the publishers.

British Library Cataloguing-in-Publication Data

A catalogue record for this book is available from the British Library.

Designed and typeset by **BKT Information Services**, Nottingham, Specialists in Desktop Publishing, Database Development, and Electronic Media Publishing.

Printed in Great Britain by Butler & Tanner Ltd, Frome and London

CONTENTS

Chapter 1:
General Employment Law 1

Chapter 2:
Redundancy 19

Chapter 3:
Unfair Dismissal 23

Chapter 4:
Sexual and Racial Discrimination 31

Chapter 5:
The National Health Service 41

Chapter 6:
NHS Trusts 45

Chapter 7:
Trade Unions 49

Appendix:
Quick Guide:
Employment Law for Nurses 56

Index 58

Central Health Studies:

The Central Health Studies (CHS) series is designed to provide nurses and other health-care professionals with up-to-date, informative texts on key professional and management issues and human skills in health care.

The Consulting Editor:

The series was conceived by John Tingle, BA Law Hons, Cert Ed, M Ed, Barrister, Senior Lecturer in Law, Nottingham Law School, Nottingham Polytechnic. John has published widely on the subject of the professional and legal accountability of health-care professionals.

The Central Health Studies Series: Published Titles

Spiritual Care: A Resource Guide

Budgeting Skills: A guide for nurse managers

Portfolio Development and Profiling for Nurses

Forthcoming Titles

Patients' Rights, Responsibilities and the Nurse

Measuring the Effectiveness of Nurse Education:
The use of performance indicators

Central Health Studies is a joint venture between **Quay Publishing Ltd.**, Lancaster and **BKT Information Services**, Nottingham

Chapter 1:
General Employment Law

Introduction.

Most practising nurses are employees, and as such are subject to general employment law, as laid down by Parliament in the Employment Protection (Consolidation) Act and elsewhere, and as established and interpreted by the courts, by Industrial Tribunals, and by the Employment Appeals Tribunal. They are also subject to the specific rules and regulations of their particular employer. These will include the Whitley Council machinery and rules within the NHS, modifications of these within NHS trusts, and a variety of different rules in the agency and private sector. Nurses who are self-employed are responsible for and to themselves in most respects, although all practising nurses, whatever their employment status, are subject to the rules of professional discipline established and administered by the United Kingdom Central Council for Nursing, Midwifery and Health Visiting (UKCC).

These cover somewhat different ground to the rules of employment law, and contain different priorities. As a result, instances are increasingly occurring where nurses find themselves trapped between a rock and a hard place as they are faced with incompatible demands from employers on the one hand, and the professional body on the other.

A later volume in this series will look specifically at the rules and procedures of the UKCC. The provisions of employment law apply to employment in all professions and all categories of employment, whether in the public or the private sector. Cases involving nurses, or for that matter other health care professionals have not been common. This is not to say that grievances and disputes do not arise, but merely that they tended to be resolved within the institution or organisation concerned, and have not been referred to a court or an industrial tribunal. Many of the cases which are relied on are therefore nothing to do with the nursing profession, but exemplify general principles which apply to every profession or employment.

It may well be that one result of the establishment of NHS Trusts, which are independent employers responsible for developing their own rules and procedures, will be a growth in contentious issues relating to employment. In the past there has been a single common industrial relations culture in the NHS, based closely on the Whitely machinery and reinforced by the existence of a national dispute and grievance procedure which gave rulings of general applicability. When employees and managers moved within the NHS, they found the same rules and, to a great extent, the same informal practices in the new establishment. NHS Trust

Employment Law

managers will no doubt draw on this common culture initially when devising employment policy for a particular trust, but divergences will inevitably develop. It will not usually make sense for a trust to develop an idiosyncratic set of employment rules (although there may be managers who are tempted to impose their personal stamp on the Trust in this way). On the other hand, just as Sainsbury and Tesco have different rules and procedures, reflecting the priorities and thinking of their managements, even though the aim is the same, namely to operate a retail sales and distribution system, so trusts will become diverse over time. One consequence of this will be the need for an employee to be alert not only to the professional content of a given post, but also the general employment policy of the employer. There may be significant differences in the attitude to job-sharing, or time off for child-rearing, as well as more tangible things like holiday entitlement. The aim of this book is to provide a general account of the law in the specific context of nursing. It is not intended as a substitute for the many manuals for lawyers, and so there is no specific reference to cases and very little to statutory provisions. It should help to explain how the law affects and shapes the environment of the workplace, but if problems arise it is essential to seek assistance from your trade union or professional association, or from a solicitor. No book can guide you through a dispute.

Employment Status

An employee enjoys substantial benefits under the law, although in many cases this is subject to satisfying qualifying conditions. These include the common law right to damages for wrongful dismissal and statutory rights to Unemployment Benefit, Statutory Sick Pay and Maternity Pay, compensation for dismissal for Redundancy, protection against Unfair Dismissal, and the right to equality of treatment on grounds of sex under both European Community Law and the Equal Pay and Sex Discrimination Acts. Common law is the body of law which has grown up over the years from general principles applied by the judges in resolving particular disputes. It thus reflects the historical development of society. Although the common law can adapt to meet new social circumstances, it does so slowly, since judges are notoriously conservative and reluctant to make precipitate changes to established rules. Statute law, on the other hand, is the body of law created by Parliament. An Act of Parliament or statute is passed with the specific intention of modernising the law or creating new rules to meet new social circumstances. This ability of Parliament to reform the law is often cited by judges as a reason for their own reluctance to depart from established rules. It must of course be remembered that whenever there is a dispute as to how the statute is to be applied or interpreted, this must be resolved by the judges in their decision in the resulting legal action. Where, as is the case with much of the statute law relating to employment, Parliament has created rules which are controversial, the attitude of the judges to the underlying policy issues will be a significant factor in the development of the law. European Community law is similar to statute law, in that it is created by the legislative organs of the European Community to deal with specific issues. It applies to all the member states of the Common Market, and is interpreted definitively by the judges of the Court of Justice of the European Communities, rather than by judges.

Some of these general rights do not apply to NHS employees, being covered by the Whitley machinery instead (*see Chapter 5*). In some case the statutory entitlements are absorbed into more generous provisions under the contract of employment. This is very commonly true in relation to sick pay.

This being so it is surprising but true that there is no clear definition of an employee. Legally the distinction is between someone who works under a contract of service (an employee) and someone who provides services to another on a self-employed basis. The position is further complicated by the fact that much employment law is now affected by European Community (EC) law. The Treaty of Rome, which is the primary source of EC law, together with various directives and regulations made under it, use the concept of the 'worker' to define those entitled to the protection of its employment law rights. It is clear that this is not simply to be equated with the various national definitions of employee status, but is a separate concept. EC law prevails over national law and must therefore be applied wherever the two are in conflict.

In the majority of cases there is no room for doubt; if a person is engaged to work at a set salary or wage, at times and on duties decided by the employer, using equipment supplied by the employer and in a way that is integrated into the employer's operation, that person is an employee. All nurses working on a permanent (or at least open-ended) basis whether in the health service or the private sector will therefore be employees. The same will however not be true of a nurse who provides services direct to patients, or who hires out her services to a series of hospitals or clinics, deciding for herself where and when she will actually work, and, in many cases, what her fee will be. Such a nurse will be self-employed, and therefore outside the scope of this book in most respects. The anti-discrimination legislation will apply to her, although not in the same way, and she does have some entitlement to Social Security benefits, although this again is on a different basis to an employee. Those rights which exist as against the employer itself will not apply because she has no employer.

What is a 'worker'?

The EC term 'worker' has been defined to the extent that the essential characteristic of a worker is that during a certain period she performs services for and under the direction of another in return for remuneration.

Employment Law

This is, in the ordinary case, going to lead to the same result as in English law, but in borderline cases there may be examples of a worker who is not an employee and vice versa.

EC employment law has two principal aspects; the first affects the rights of individual workers in their ordinary place of employment, and these points are discussed where they arise during the course of the book. They effectively supplement or modify pre-existing national rules, although a recent case in the European Court of Justice has gone beyond this by stating that in cases where the home country has failed to bring in regulations required by an EC directive, a worker who suffers a loss as a result may be entitled to claim damages from the home state. The second aspect relates to rights of free movement within the EC to seek and take up work or to set up in independent practice, mutual recognition of educational and professional qualifications, and transferability of social security provisions. These will form the subject matter of a future companion volume. It should be noted that EC rights apply only to EC nationals.

The English Law tests

It is necessary to consider how cases which fall in the grey area between clear cases of employee status and clear cases of self-employment are resolved by the courts. The question can be important for a number of reasons. Because the social security benefits available to the self-employed are less extensive than those for employees (no unemployment benefit for example), the self-employed contribution is lower than that of the employed earner, and of course there is no employer to pay a contribution at all. There is thus an incentive for the parties concerned to categorise the arrangement as self-employment so the worker pays less and the person for whom the work is done pays nothing, and for the Department of Social Security to categorise it as employment. The provider of work also has the incentive that those doing the work will not be entitled to assert any of the rights against him that an employee would have. In this case the interests of the parties are, of course, opposed. Finally the point has arisen because in law the employer is liable to compensate those injured by the negligence of an employee acting in the course of her employment (technically known as vicarious liability), but is not liable under normal circumstances to compensate those injured by a self employed person or 'independent contractor'.

The courts have, over the years, devised a series of tests to distinguish employment from self employment. One early one was to consider whether there was power to control what work was done, when, where and how it was done. If so, the person doing the work was an employee. This test is somewhat difficult to apply to a professional person, especially if she is working for someone who is not herself in the same profession. It becomes almost impossible to apply to, say, a community nurse who is very much responsible for organising her own timetable, as well as taking professional responsibility for her patients. A test devised somewhat later is whether the person doing the work is integrated into the undertaking concerned, or is simply making a specific input from time to time as required. This test would certainly assist to categorise the community nurse as an employee. It does, however, provide little guidance in relation to, among others, those who regularly work for two or three different enterprises. The present approach is to consider all the aspects of the relationship in question. The categorisation of the arrangement by the parties themselves is taken into account, but is not conclusive. The fact the work must be done personally (i.e. it cannot be delegated) is a strong indicator of employment. Where there is substantial equipment needed, it will be an indication of employment if it is the employer who supplies and maintains this. If the person doing the work is free to accept or reject particular assignments and/or to work for others, this will be an indication of self employment. Payment by assignment, rather than by time spent, also indicates self employment, but is not a very strong indicator. The task of the judge is to ascertain which of these, and other, factors, are present in the particular case, and to weigh them all up. The conclusion is therefore the result of a balancing exercise taking account of all relevant factors. One important aspect of this exercise is to look at how the parties to the agreement describe the effect of the agreement. It must, however, be stressed that this description is not conclusive. As the judges have said, discussing similar problems in another field of law, the fact that the parties to an agreement choose to call a digging implement with a broad, flat, metal blade a fork, will not prevent the court from saying that they are, in fact, describing a spade. So the courts may rule that an agreement which the parties describe as creating self-employed status actually creates that of employment, or *vice versa*.

Working for an agency

Many nurses work for agencies. The business of the agency is to supply staff to hospitals, or home nurses for patients. Such arrangements are legally complex. The nurse may be self-employed, and in this case her contract may be with the agency or the end user of her services. On the other hand she may be employed, either by the agency or by the end user. In any event, she will be subject to the instructions of the nursing and management hierarchy within a hospital, and will owe a personal duty of care to all patients for whom she is responsible. Normally the legal position is in fact regulated by the documents produced by the agency for its dealings with the nurse and the end user respectively. It is probably fair to say that most nurses (and indeed the other parties to the arrangement) do not give much thought to the legal position, but it is significant. It is important of course for the nurse to know what her legal status is, so that she knows, for instance, who, if anyone, owes her the obligations of an employer. But it may also be important for others. If the nurse has been negligent, will the claim lie against her as an independent practitioner, against the hospital as employer or against the agency as employer. The patient will want to know who to sue. On the other hand, who is responsible for insurance? As mentioned earlier, any nurse owes her patient a duty of care. In other words, she must be expected at all times to look after them with the care and skill to be expected of the reasonable nurse. This duty can be broken in many ways, ranging from physical clumsiness (perhaps resulting in dropping a patient) through careless inattention to the task in hand (perhaps resulting in the administration of the wrong drug or an overdose) to a failure to follow proper professional standards (perhaps a call in a doctor at the appropriate stage if a patient is deteriorating or some anomaly manifests itself). If there is a breach of this duty and the patient suffers harm, which will usually be pain and suffering, but which may include loss of earnings and other similar financial losses, then the patient can sue for damages. Such claims, while not particularly common, are on the increase. They are extremely costly to deal with. The legal costs, including the cost of expert evidence to establish exactly what happened and whether it was a breach of duty, can be very high, especially if the case is a complex one. The normal rule is that the losing party in the case pays the winning party's costs. The risk is thus virtually doubled. However, in all cases the basis on which the costs are awarded is such that a proportion of the costs are not in fact paid. Also, in some cases the losing party cannot pay, whether or not ordered to do so. The highest awards for damages are now substantially over one million pounds. While such cases are extremely rare, they do occur. It is thus vital to ensure that there is adequate insurance to deal with any claim that may be made. Otherwise the nurse involved faces financial ruin. Where the nurse is employed, the employer is vicariously liable for her actions, and one would expect the claim to be made against the employer, and dealt with by the employer or his insurer. Where the nurse is self employed, she needs her own insurance cover. All prospective agency nurses should check the insurance position carefully, and ensure the position is satisfactory.

The Contract of Employment

We have already referred to employment as being a contract of service, and the basis of the employment relationship is indeed a contract, that is a voluntary agreement between employer and employee to trade work and skill for remuneration. In theory, employer and employee specifically agree all the terms and conditions at the outset of the employment relationship. In practice this is not the case. Some matters are indeed agreed, although in addition to express agreement there may be terms impliedly agreed on. These will be matters which, according to custom and practice, routinely apply to employment of this type, and which therefore did not need to be specifically mentioned, although both parties would have unhesitatingly accepted them if proposed by the other or by a third party. Other terms (such as the Whitley agreements) between employers and trade unions and professional associations regulating such issues as salaries on a local or national basis for all employees in a given category. In the case of the NHS, the collective bargaining machinery for salaries has been abolished and replaced by a review body, which operates under statutory authority. The actual pay award is thus not negotiated in the traditional way. Once made it is however incorporated in a similar way into individual contracts.

Yet other terms are regulated by Parliament. The Employment Protection (Consolidation) Act lays down (among many other things) minimum periods of notice which actually override anything actually agreed, while the Equal Pay Act incorporates an 'equality clause' into every contract of employment. This means that in any given case the actual wishes of employer and employee are relatively unimportant, and it is necessary to consider these general factors in addition in order to understand fully the totality of the rights and obligations created by the particular employment relationship. It is also necessary to bear in mind that the law of contract generally concerns itself with one-off transactions, such as sales of goods, and there are difficulties in applying rules designed for this situation to a long-term relationship which is dynamic in the sense that the expectations and intentions of the parties will change over time, often in ways that are hard to predict and provide for in advance. This has caused particular problems in relation to changes in the terms and conditions of employment. Changing economic, political or technical conditions may lead the employer to wish to alter the terms of employment; these changes may not be welcome to the employee. The changes will be made to the individual contract of the particular employee, but will probably affect a class of employees, who may respond collectively through a trade union or professional association, but who may have conflicting wishes. Serious difficulties can arise, especially in relation to the question whether the employer is entitled to insist on imposing changes, either because he impliedly has the right to make alterations under a flexibility provision, or because he can terminate the existing contract and offer a new one on the revised terms.

Form of the Contract

There is no generally applicable compulsory form of contract of employment. Indeed the contract does not even have to be in writing. Within thirteen weeks of the commencement of employment the employer must give to the employee a written statement of the principal terms and conditions of employment, but this does not have to contain the whole contract, although sometimes the employer chooses to have it do so. Sometimes this takes the form of a letter of appointment, while some employers use standard forms. This is perfectly acceptable, as is the common practice of setting out matters applying equally to all employees, such as sick pay rules and grievance and disciplinary procedures in separate documents. These are either displayed for the employee to read, or copies are provided. A similar procedure is followed where the provisions of a collective agreement are incorporated in the contract of employment. The intention is that any employee should be able to work out her rights and responsibilities by reference to documents in her possession or to which she has ready access, and will therefore be able to enforce those rights if necessary.

Although the employer should provide written information, as set out above, it must be stressed that there will be a contract even where this done. The problem in such cases is to work out what the terms of the contract are. The Industrial Tribunal has jurisdiction to establish what the terms of the contract are, although only in a case where it is necessary to do so in order to settle some problem of substance. Employees often think that, because they do not have a formal contract, or at least some documentary evidence of a contract, that they do not have a contract of employment. This is emphatically not the case. It is of course desirable for there to be some appropriate documentation, since this makes it much easier for the parties to know what their rights and responsibilities are, but it is not legally necessary. The contract results from the acceptance of the offer of employment, and obligations exist on both sides at that stage which may, of course, be some time before the employee actually starts work.

The specific provisions of any particular contract, or the general terms and conditions of any employer (and while the NHS is governed in general terms by the Whitley machinery, each health authority has its own terms and conditions which differ in detail) need to be considered in detail before their effect can be explained. This detailed analysis is beyond the scope of this book. In most cases, disputes on the meaning of a particular clause are of no help when looking at a similar clause which adopts a different form of words.

Implied terms

The remarks above apply to matters which are expressly stated in the contract or are incorporated by reference to particular documents. There are also obligations which are imposed on both parties to the contract without being spelled out expressly. Some of these are brought into play by statute as outlined above, but others owe their origin to the decisions of courts over the years as to obligations which are so fundamental and essential that they apply even if they have not been specifically incorporated.

The principal such obligation on the employer is to treat employees with reasonable courtesy and consideration and also with reasonable regard for each employee's personal circumstances so far as these are or ought to be known to the employer. The employer is also responsible for the actions of fellow employees to the extent that it has instructed them to act in a particular way or sits back and does nothing in relation to complaints. One common area for the application of this principle is in the field of sexual harassment. If the employer is made aware that one employee is harassing others and fails to take effective steps to discipline him or otherwise remedy the situation, it may be liable, even though the acts complained of are forbidden. If the harasser is a senior manager, then his actions may be treated as those of the employing organisation itself. If he is a junior employee, the employer will only be responsible if it has facilitated or condoned his behaviour. In a case a few years ago, a female employee successfully claimed because the employer had failed to take effective action in response to her complaints that her female colleagues were distressing her by publicly discussing details of their rather lurid sex lives. The principle would also apply where an employer had refused or failed to take child care and other personal responsibilities into account when working out a duty roster.

It must be stressed that the duty on the employer is to act reasonably; the employer is not responsible for every casual piece of offensive behaviour by colleagues, only for institutional behaviour or a course of conduct that could be controlled. Likewise, the employer can ultimately place operational requirements before the convenience of staff, but only after proper investigation. One matter which will shortly need to be resolved is the extent to which this implied duty requires the employer to have regard to the responsibilities of a professionally qualified employee to work in accordance with the professional standards established by the relevant professional body. The possibility of a conflict between the requirements of the employer and those of the professional body has already been mentioned, but the issue appears to have arisen in practice largely in relation to confidentiality and whistle-blowing, which is discussed below, rather than in the context of a positive obligation on the employer.

Employees are under two principal implied obligations. The first is one of loyalty. Most of the cases which have arisen have been in commerce and industry and involved the leaking or misuse of trade secrets or other commercially sensitive information. There is a general duty not to disclose confidential information. This is often reinforced nowadays with a specific obligation not to discuss matters relating to employment with outsiders, especially the media. This has raised serious issues of professional responsibility, where the attempt to prevent public dissemination of information has related directly to issues of patient care, since the duty to the employer appears to be in direct conflict with the obligation imposed on all practitioners by clause 11 of the UKCC Code of Professional Conduct to '*report to appropriate person or authority, having regard to the physical, psychological, and social effects on patients and clients, any circumstances in the environment of care which could jeopardise standards of practice,*' and the further obligation in clause 12 to '*report to appropriate person or authority any circumstances in which safe and appropriate care for patients and clients cannot be provided.*'. Obviously the appropriate initial approach must be to management within the employing organisation. They are in the best position to recognise and remedy any problem. The problem arises if management fail to deal with the complaint in a satisfactory manner. The nurse in the case is on the horns of a dilemma. Remaining silent may result in disciplinary proceedings for failure to defend the interests of patients or colleagues, while speaking out may result in disciplinary action. The best known such case is that of nurse Graham Pink. Nurse Pink was concerned that staffing levels at the hospital where he was employed were inadequate, and that the safety and comfort of patients were thereby at risk. He initially aired his concerns internally but did not receive a response which was satisfactory to him. It appears that there was a difference of professional opinion between him and the hospital management, and as a result his complaints were not accepted as valid. Nurse Pink then elected to publicise his concerns in an article in *The Guardian* which aroused considerable public concern and comment, much of it adverse to the management of the hospital. This resulted in disciplinary action on the grounds of breach of confidentiality both with regard to the hospital and one of the patients. The outcome of these proceedings are now in turn being challenged in the law courts. Once these proceedings have been decided we should have some guidance as the balance to be struck between these competing demands. The recent declaration by the Secretary of State for Health protecting whistle blowers in the Health Authority sector is intended to remove this threat, but it remains to be seen whether this will be seen as an effective deterrent.

The second implied obligation is one requiring the employee to act reasonably to further the employer's operations. This entails, on the one hand, flexibility and on the other, professionalism. A rigid adherence to the rules, particularly in the form of a 'work to rule' in pursuance of an industrial dispute may be seen as a breach of this obligation if the result is not to operate the rules as intended to ensure the safety of oneself, colleagues and patients, but to bring the operation to a stand-still. This would probably apply to a 'work to grade' within the NHS if it entailed, for example a wilfully pedantic interpretation of such notions as 'direct supervision.' The duty to act professionally owed to the employer overlaps with that imposed by the UKCC Code. In this instance there is no blatant conflict between the two, although there may be problem areas. An employer may ask a nurse to fulfil duties proper to a higher grade on a temporary basis because of staff absences or other urgent reasons. The employer would regard it as unprofessional to refuse, although this would in turn depend on the specific skills required and those which the nurse has, while the UKCC would consider the effect on patient care rather than organisational considerations. This duty certainly does not require an employee to carry out duties appropriate to a higher grade on a long-term

General

basis. Much of the bitterness associated with the implementation of the regrading of nursing posts at the end of the 1980s arose because the number of high-grade posts was limited by financial constraints and was less than the number of posts which deserved the higher grade. Once the employer had established the grading criteria, it was arguably a breach of their duty to treat employees with reasonable consideration to expect staff to accept the salary of a lower grade for doing a job with a higher grade specification.

Express terms

The terms incorporated under the Whitley machinery will be discussed in the chapter on that subject. In other cases, the express terms will vary in detail. Some variations will follow from the circumstances of the particular employee, such as the job description, while others will depend on the policy of the particular employer. It follows that in a general account of the law, it is not possible to explain how every term in a contract should be drafted. This section should therefore be considered as a general guide, rather than as a specific drafting template for a particular contract. It should however indicate what areas need to be covered.

The parties. It is important to know exactly who the employer is, especially if there are several companies or organisations operating from the same premises, and also whether there is continuity of employment from an earlier post with the same employer or an associated employer.

Job description. Normally, an employee is required to perform the duties of the job as described; it may be necessary to go beyond this on occasion in the interests of flexibility, or if there is an emergency, but the employee should know what is required of her. The job description should be reviewed periodically, particularly in smaller institutions, which tend to be more informal, and where a significant change in responsibilities may take place over time without being reflected in the regrading or change of job description.

Place of employment. It is now common practice for employers with an extensive operation, such as most district health authorities, to state that employees will be based a named site, but may be required to work at any site as needed. This has implications for the employee, who may be required to change her usual routine, and also for the employer, who cannot claim that the employee is redundant simply on the basis of the situation at the normal place of work.

Rates of pay. If the salary is individually negotiated, the basic rate and mechanism for review must be spelled out. If there is a salary scale, then the starting point in the scale must be stated. In all cases, the position with regard to extra work must be clear. The employee's entitlement may be to overtime, or to time in lieu. The law does not prescribe which, or the periods for which premium rates of pay (e.g. for work at unsocial hours, or on public holidays) will be given. All these matters must therefore be covered.

Hours of Work. The law does not stipulate the length of a working week, or when hours are to be worked. If there is a shift system, or arrangements for flexi-time, these will need to be spelled out.

Other benefits. The contract should deal with any allowances, whether in cash or in kind, such as travelling expenses, contributions to telephone costs, and provision of clothes or equipment. If these represent anything other than the reimbursement of money actually laid out, there will be income tax implications (the obvious example is the provision of a vehicle).

Holidays and sickness. The contract should specify the amount of holiday and when it should be taken. There are often detailed rules about taking holidays within a given holiday year, and for booking leave. The law does not make any general provisions for this, so it is essential that the contract covers it, otherwise there will be great scope for disagreement. While there are detailed statutory rules for sick pay and sickleave (and also for pay and leave for maternity, which is similar in that it causes absence from duty), it is often the case that the parties have agreed something different.

It is of course common to find that holiday and sickness arrangements, together with such things as disciplinary rules and grievance procedures are set out in generally applicable documents, and these need only be dealt with specifically if there is to be a particular variation an individual case. On the other hand, there is an almost infinite number of special provisions which may apply to a particular job, and which should be spelled out at the outset. Some of these will be of a temporary nature (such as an agreement to honour existing holiday commitments when starting work), but they are not always so, such as an agreement to provide facilities or sponsorship for education or training.

Relationship of Express and Implied terms

The traditional view of the law has been that express terms, where they exist, will prevail over any suggested implied term. The theory is that an implied term is simply the term which the parties would have put in if they had been asked to specifically consider the point. It follows that where they have expressed themselves, this must be at the expense of the 'usual' implied terms. This view of implied terms can seem artificial, but this will not necessarily persuade the courts to abandon it. One area where problems will arise is where the express term and the implied term do not cover the same area. A good example is the implied term requiring the employer to respect the professional obligations of the employee as compared to an express term preventing the employee from commenting publicly on matters relating to the employer's affairs. There is clearly a degree of overlap, as has been discussed above. It is at present unclear how these

General

problems will be resolved. In theory, the law should secure and maintain a fair balance between the private right of the employer to maintain a fair balance between the private right of the employer to ensure the confidentiality of information relating to its business affairs and the public interest right to be advised of abuses. In practice, the judges have tended to protect and enforce the private right at the expense of the public one, since the employer has a clear and explicit contractual term on which it can rely, and indeed can be seen as owning the information in question, while the public interest right rests on much more nebulous considerations. Under English law, rights of property have always enjoyed a high degree of protection. It could be argued that the express non-disclosure clause should be read as being itself limited to situations where it is the employer's commercial confidentiality which is at issue, or as not requiring the employee to keep silent about life-threatening abuses, or indeed as not applying to matters within the scope of the professional duty, but any such approach would require the court to rewrite the clause, and courts are reluctant to do this. There is also the possibility that the court may hold that the professional duty is satisfied by a report to the employer, and that it does not extend to public whistle-blowing. It is therefore far from certain that the law as it stands will provide an answer to the question which is acceptable to those who regard professional and public obligations as paramount.

Varying the contract

The common law has always been uneasy at any suggestion that a contract should be varied over time. Parliament has been prepared to intervene in the workings of the contract to a much greater extent. Most contracts are set up to cover a single transaction, and once there is agreement it will only be in rare cases that it needs to be altered. A contract of employment, particularly an open-ended one, is intended to regulate the relationship between the employer and employee over a long period. Changes are inevitable. Salary scales will be revised in line with inflation and other factors. Hours of work will be altered, as will job descriptions. The employer may well wish to change his disciplinary procedure or the holiday scheme. In some case it is assumed, quite reasonably, that there is a mutual consent to the substitution of new terms. This would apply where the pay rise has been negotiated. The new salary scales are substituted for the old. The employer will be allowed to change his general rules and regulations; these do not form part of the contract of employment, but are a part of the organisation of the undertaking. Such changes cannot extend beyond this. It is not normally the case that the employer can change the actual terms of the contract unilaterally without consent. It may be that if changes are introduced and tacitly accepted, this will be treated as consent, but it is the case that the attempt to impose new conditions can be resisted by the employee. The employer is in essence refusing to be bound by the

Employment Law

existing contract; this is a breach of that contract and may well constitute a constructive dismissal. In practice, however, the employee may have little choice but to accept the change. If the employer demonstrates that the change is necessary for the proper functioning of his undertaking, any such constructive dismissal will be held to be fair within the meaning of the legislation (*See Chapter 3*). The employee will find herself without a job, and probably without compensation for losing it. The usual practice is, of course, for such changes to be negotiated between trade unions and management, so that the unacceptable points are removed before they are put into force.

Termination of Employment

Many disputes, whether as to terms and conditions, or of a disciplinary nature, do not result in resignation or dismissal, but as most of the cases which have been worth arguing in the courts and Industrial Tribunals have involved termination, it is usual to discuss these issues in that context.

The Contractual Position

The position being described here is the one which exists as a result of a contract of employment being entered into as an agreement between the two parties, employer and employee. It takes no account of the modern statutory rules on employment protection, which are considered later. The present rules (technically known as the common law rules) are the basis on which the statutory rules are founded. They still apply where the statutory rules do not, and co-exist with them in other cases; it is however important to remember that they usually do not provide the complete answer, and the statutory rules must also be taken into account. In addition to the terms of the contract, which as we have seen have been actually or notionally agreed between the parties, it is necessary to consider other rules and requirements of the employer. There is a crucial distinction between the two things. The terms of the contract give rights and responsibilities to both parties and can, in theory, by varied only by consent. The employer does, however, have the right to manage his business and its affairs, and one of the aspects of management in this sense is the right to make rules and regulations, and to set up management structures and systems. Some of these will not impinge directly on employees, but others will. A change in the staffing of a particular function, or in the procedures for recording presence at work will have a direct impact in this way, as will changes in health and safety procedures. The employer is, as a matter of contractual obligation, perfectly free to make such changes, subject only to the implied term requiring reasonable consideration for employees. A rule change which had an unreasonable and adverse effect upon employees might amount to a breach of that term, as might a failure to consult those affected or discuss the changes. Such consultation is normally regarded as part of good industrial relations practice. It must, however, be stressed that it is the

General

procedure for rule changes which requires the employer to consult and take account of the interests of the employees. The substance of the change is finally a matter for the employer alone, and can be imposed even in the absence of an agreement. Whether the employer regards it as expedient to implement unpopular changes in this way is a separate question.

The actual agreement will either be for a fixed term, long or short, or on an open-ended basis, terminable on reasonable notice. Fixed-term contracts used to be rare but they are now much more common. They are used for managers to assist in defining the time within which specific objectives must be achieved, and in other contexts largely to avoid the creation of a large and inflexible permanent staff. When the fixed term expires, or proper notice is given the contract comes to an end. Neither party has any grievance in law, since this is what the contract provided for and it is a fulfilment of the original agreement. A similar result occurs when the parties mutually agree to end the employment prematurely. In practice, of course, one or other party may well have a grievance in fact, if an open-ended contract is ended on notice. The employee may have no other job to go to, and conversely the employer may not be able to replace the departing employee. These inconveniences are seen as irrelevant by the common law; they are simply facts of economic and social life. The law does however regard a premature termination of employment (except by agreement) as being a breach of the original agreement, and this will give the injured party a right to compensation and possibly other remedies. There are a number of problem areas in this regard:

- Normally the length of notice required will be spelt out in the written particulars of the contract; failing this there are statutory minimum periods laid down. There are however cases where there is nothing expressly agreed, but it is claimed that the statutory minima do not reflect the reasonable expectation of the aggrieved party, usually the employee. If nothing is specified there is a right to reasonable notice. In a case of disagreement, the length of this will have to be determined by a court. The normal approach is to consider custom and practice in the profession.
- In some cases an employee may be prevented from working by ill-health or other reasons outside their control (e.g. imprisonment). The contract will often make specific provision for ill-health; it is generally accepted that where there is provision for sick pay, the employer acknowledges that absence for periods within the limits of sick pay entitlement are within the scope of the contract and do not give rise to a right to terminate it. If the contract is silent, the court will have to determine what length of absence should reasonably be accepted in this way. Longer absences, and extended absences

for other reasons will probably result in a finding that the contract of employment is frustrated. This is a technical legal term; it means that it is no longer possible to give effect to the basic purpose of the contract (in this case that the employee will work for the employer), and that this has happened without fault (in the sense of a wilful breach of contractual obligations on either side). The legal result is that the contract is at an end, but as it has happened without fault, no compensation is payable. It should be noted that the courts are reluctant to treat contracts of employment as frustrated. Very long periods of absence have been held not to have this effect, both in cases where the employee was one of a number in a pool of staff, on the basis that the available work could be redistributed, and also in the case of senior and highly trained staff on the basis that finding and training a replacement would take so long that it was more logical to await the return of the existing employee. Applying the same reasoning to an employee with a key job in a small team which is not particularly specialised, would suggest that early replacement was justified.

Justifying premature termination of the contract

If one party has gravely breached their obligations under the contract, this may entitle the other to treat the contract as at an end. This takes the form of a resignation or dismissal without notice (often called 'summary dismissal'). Most of the cases concern summary dismissal rather than resignation without notice. To justify summary dismissal the employer must prove that the employee has been guilty of gross misconduct. This will include dishonesty in relation to the employer, gross insubordination or violent conduct on duty and, in the nursing context, abuse of drugs, violence towards or abuse of patients and gross negligence. It should be noted that the situation is one of 'all or nothing'. Either the behaviour amounts to gross misconduct or it does not. There is no question of the employee being held partly to blame for misconduct which falls short of being gross, and having her remedies restricted accordingly. Once the court has determined that there has indeed been a breach of contract, it proceeds to consider what remedy is required.

The normal remedy is damages. These are designed to put the injured party into the position they would have been in if the contract had been performed. Usually this means a payment equal to the net difference between the amount actually received and the amount which would have been received had the contract been terminated on the earliest date on which this could legally be done. This approximates to wages in lieu of notice.

The calculation should take account of the value of fringe benefits or in the modern jargon the 'total remuneration package.' Net figures must be used as damages are not taxable.

There is a duty to mitigate the loss by seeking alternative employment. Any earnings during the notice period will be set against damages. Damages may be reduced if the court is satisfied that the employee has made no genuine effort to find work.

Where some notice is given, but it is not legally sufficient, the claim relates only to the balance of the notice period.

There is no claim for annoyance and distress at the manner of the dismissal, or for other side-issues such as the effect on career prospects, except in the special case where the contract broken was a training contract specifically linked to a particular qualification.

Employers rarely pursue employees who leave without proper notice. The law will not force the employee back to work, although it may prevent her from working for someone else if she had promised not to. This situation is unlikely to affect the ordinary nurse, but it may affect senior and managerial staff going to work for rival organisations, especially in the private sector. The restriction will only be for the limited period necessary to protect the first employer's legitimate interests, often six or twelve months. An order of this kind will not be made if it is an indirect way of forcing the employee back to the original employer, but this is rare; the nurse could always work outside nursing for the period of the restriction. A claim for damages is of limited value to an employer. The employee will probably not be worth pursuing, except to be made an example of, and in any case the employer must show an actual loss. He will have saved the employee's salary, and this should cover paying a replacement.

Statutory Notice

As already mentioned there are minimum periods laid down which override anything actually agreed. The notice rules only apply to open-ended contracts.

An employee must give a week's notice after being employed for four weeks or longer.

An employer must give one week's notice during the first two years of employment, and thereafter one week's notice for each complete year of employment, up to a maximum of twelve weeks. The statutory notice provisions do not affect dismissal for gross misconduct.

Continuity of Employment

Many of the statutory rights associated with employment apply only to employees who have completed a specified period of continuous employment either with the same employer or with two or more associated employers, and the value of those rights may vary with the total length of

Employment Law

such service. Both 'continuous employment' and 'associated employer' are technical terms and must be construed accordingly.

Continuous employment means employment that has not been broken or terminated, and under a contract which normally entails at least sixteen hours work per week.

Exceptionally once an employee has worked for five years under a contract which normally entails at least eight hours work a week, this will qualify as continuous employment.

Sickness, holidays and strikes do not break continuity, although it should be noted that any period on strike will not count towards a qualifying period.

Associated employers are any two or more undertakings or organisations which are within the same group or controlled by the same person. The definition does not apply to the constituent parts of the NHS or to NHS trusts. It can apply in the private sector, or in some instances in local government.

Excercises

1. What benefits are due to employees under:
   a) Common Law;
   b) Statute Law?

2. What criteria are used to distinguish an employee from a self-employed person?

3. List the pros and cons of being:
   a) An employee;
   b) A self-employed person.

4. Look at your own employment status. Are you:
   a) employed or self-employed?
   b) If employed, who is your employer?
   c) If you work for an agency, what is your insurance situation?

Chapter 2: Redundancy

General meaning

In common parlance redundancy arises when an employee's job disappears because the employer goes out of business, moves away or undergoes a major reorganisation. Originally if this happened it was just bad luck. Even the most long-serving employee was entitled to nothing more than proper notice or payment in lieu, and even this would not be forthcoming if the former employer was insolvent. There was nothing to stop employers and employees from negotiating arrangements for severance pay, and this was done to some extent. The Whitley machinery covered employees of the NHS, and this scheme is still in operation. NHS employees are, therefore, not covered by the statutory scheme. NHS trust employees will initially be covered by the Whitley scheme. There are still employers who operate severance pay schemes in parallel with the statutory scheme; such schemes provide enhanced benefits, but each must be considered in the light of its own rules.

The Statutory Scheme

This dates back to 1965. It was the first substantial intervention by Parliament into individual employment law in modern times. The principle is that an employee who is redundant is entitled to a payment calculated by reference to age, salary and length of service. This is intended to reflect the employee's 'investment' of time and energy in the job. Although largely paid by the employer there are mechanisms for ensuring that payment is made even where the employer is insolvent. As one might expect, there are definitions of the various terms in order to clarify exactly who qualifies for a payment and the amount.

Redundancy defined

An employee is redundant for statutory purposes if, and only, if they are dismissed primarily because:

- The employer has ceased to carry on the business for the purposes of which the employee was employed or intends to do so shortly; or
- The requirements of that business for employees to carry out work of the particular kind which the employee was employed to perform have ceased or diminished or are expected to do so.

In either case the situation may affect the business as a whole or simply the location where the employee was based.

The statutory definition therefore covers on the one hand a closure of the operation, whether total or partial, and on the other hand a reorganisation which entails the loss of certain skills and types of workers and their replacement by others. By way of example, the closure of a private hospital or nursing home comes into the first category, while a change from an orthodox care home to a specialised psycho-geriatric unit comes into the second.

An employer cannot avoid creating a redundancy situation by regularly or repeatedly laying off staff temporarily or putting them on short time working. There is a formula to establish a point at which this is regarded as equivalent to notice of redundancy, although the onus is on the employees affected to elect to treat it as such and claim a redundancy payment. They may, if they can see a return to normality ahead, prefer to accept the situation and wait for better times. If they do so, they are entitled to guarantee payments for days not worked, but the amount of these is only at (approximately) benefit levels. There is no obligation to pay full wages.

Where there are substantial redundancies in prospect, the employer is obliged to consult with any recognised trade union or similar body. Failure to do so will result in additional compensation (a protective award) being made to those affected.

The scheme only applies to those who are employed to work in the UK.

Some employees have contracts of employment which contain either an express or an implied mobility clause. This means that although they normally work at a particular place, they can be required to work elsewhere, either at other specified sites, or generally. In this case there will be no redundancy if there is a suitable post available within the organisation, as where one unit is closed, but similar posts are offered in another somewhere else. If the employee does not take the new post up, perhaps because it is personally inconvenient, this is, strictly, not a redundancy, although the difference is sometimes fudged over when there are a number of posts to be lost overall.

On the other hand, where there is a mobility clause, the onus is on the employer to consider whether there are other posts within the organisation (including any associated employers) which are within the employee's contract. If this is not done, there may be a claim for unfair dismissal.

Selection for redundancy

It is often necessary to select some members of a group of employees for redundancy. This must be done on a basis which is fair and objective. There must first be a call for volunteers. If it is necessary to declare compulsory redundancies this is to be done on the basis of criteria which have been established in advance (either as part of the general industrial

Redundancy

relations machinery for that organisation, or by negotiation in the particular case). The traditional criterion was length of service or 'Last In–First Out.' Employers argue that this is unreasonable because it may require them to keep the unfit, incompetent and uncooperative and dismiss younger, more enthusiastic employees who are essential to the future prosperity of the organisation. It is therefore permissible to select on the basis of efficiency criteria, provided these are clearly laid down, objectively justifiable, and there is evidence to prove that they are being applied even handedly. In other words the criteria must not be open to abuse in order to get rid of undesirables.

This problem is compounded in the case of reorganisations affecting professional or managerial staff. These typically entail the establishment of a new structure, with fewer posts overall, but each post being new in the sense that it has a new job description. If the change is minor, it can be argued that it is the old one under a new name and the post-holder should retain it. Where the changes are more substantial there may be real doubt as to which posts in the old scheme have been made redundant. Again the onus is on the employer to show that the selection for redundancy has been made on objective criteria, as listed above, although in this case the relevance of the qualifications and experience of the members of the affected 'pool' of employees to fulfil the duties of the new posts can legitimately be taken into account.

Redundancy Payments

These are available to employees aged 20 or over and under 65 who can show two years continuous service. They are made in respect of a period of service of up to 20 years, counting back from the date of termination. Any longer period is ignored. The payment is based on a week's pay. There are rules to calculate this to allow for fluctuations, and there is a relatively low statutory maximum figure, which is normally reviewed annually. The rate of payment is half a week's pay for qualifying years starting when the claimant was aged 18–21, one week's pay for such years when aged 22–40, and one and a half week's pay for such years aged 41–64.

There will be no right to a redundancy payment if the employer offers suitable alternative employment and the employee unreasonably turns this down. This is not the same as the situation described above where, because of a mobility clause, there is no redundancy; it covers cases where the employer is willing to retrain employees, or to offer work in other locations which are not covered by a mobility clause. There are provisions for a trial period in the new job, and the employee's personal circumstances are taken into account when deciding if it was reasonable to turn down the alternative employment.

Employment Law

The Whitley Scheme

This scheme, contained in Section 45 of the general agreement, is closely based on the statutory scheme, but provides certain additional benefits. The normal maximum payment is 30 weeks' pay, available in the same circumstances as the statutory payment. However, the employee is entitled to take a week's pay as 7/365*ths* of annual salary if that is more than the normal statutory calculation (thus avoiding the statutory ceiling), and there is a provision for gaps of service of up to 12 months to be ignored when calculating statutory service. Service with any Health Service Authority will count. Payments are made to those with two or more years' continuous service, or five or more years continuous part-time service (as defined in each case in Chapter One). There is a provision for an an enhanced payments to those over 41, who get an additional two weeks' pay per year of service aged 18 and over up to a maximum of 50 weeks (or 25 years), and an additional two weeks' pay per year of service aged 41 and over up to a maximum of 16 weeks. The maximum total payment is therefore 66 weeks' pay. This is, however, subject to the proviso that the employee does not immediately receive superannuation payments under the early retirement scheme. Section 46 of the general agreement, together with various DHSS and health department department circulars make detailed provisions for advanced and enhanced superannuation where there is early retirement for redundancy, organisational changes, or 'in the interests of the service', typically on grounds of limited efficiency.

The right to a redundancy payment is lost if suitable alternative employment with a Health Service Authority is accepted or is unreasonably refused. There are criteria for the reasonable of a refusal; these seem largely to turn on geographic location. An employee is expected to move within a six-mile radius without compensation, and further if travelling or relocation expenses are paid. There is no guarantee of a similar post, although it must be a reasonable one having regard to the employee's capabilities and experience. Family ties, such as a partner's employment, children's schooling or commitments as a carer are not explicitly acknowledged as valid reasons for refusing a transfer to another area. In practice, they are acknowledged as they are under the statutory scheme.

Exercises

1. Does your contract of employment include an express or implied mobility clause?

2. If you were asked to transfer to an establishment in a city 500 miles from where you work to do the same job, what would be your legal situation if you refused the move?

Chapter 3:
Unfair Dismissal

The General Scheme

In Chapter 1 we considered the remedy which the common law provides to an employee who claims that her contract for employment has been improperly terminated—the claim for damages for wrongful dismissal. In the first place, if the employer gives proper notice, he is acting quite lawfully under these rules. If he does not, all the law requires i that he pays damages equal to salary in lieu of notice. There is no claim to reinstatement, and therefore no protection of the actual job. An employer could therefore dismiss an employee for any reason or none, provided she worked or was paid for the notice period. In 1971, a statutory remedy for unfair dismissal was introduced. The intention was that reinstatement should be the primary remedy where there was a successful application, but in practice most successful cases result in an order for compensation. It was also the intention that cases should be dealt with in a relatively informal manner; here too the reality has been that many cases have been long and the legal arguments as to the interpretation of the legislation have been complex and subtle. The result is that the whole area is now highly technical, and expert legal advice is needed to pursue a claim. Even the word 'unfair' has acquired a technical meaning far removed from its everyday one. Unfair dismissal claims are not heard by the ordinary courts, but by Industrial Tribunals, from which there is a right of appeal to the Employment Appeal Tribunal.

Although wrongful and unfair dismissal are both concerned with the same underlying problem, namely whether an employer has improperly terminated an employee's employment, each is based on different principles and rules. A given dismissal may be:

- Both wrongful and unfair, as where there is summary dismissal for no reason or, more likely, for an obviously trivial reason (e.g. a first instance of lateness or absenteeism).
- Unfair but not wrongful, where, although the grounds alleged are inadequate, proper notice was given (e.g. a situation similar to that given above, but where dismissal is on proper notice).
- Fair but wrongful. This is a relatively rare category. It covers cases where there is a summary dismissal and, although there is an acceptable reason for dismissal (as described below), it does not amount to gross misconduct (e.g. an employee who is incompetent and has been given the necessary warnings and

additional training or support). In such cases there is no real justification for a summary dismissal.
- Fair and non-wrongful. This applies where there is gross misconduct and the employer also investigates it properly, or where there is a necessary degree of fault and proper notice is given (e.g. a situation like that given immediately above, but where notice is given).

As with redundancy, the legislation only applies to those employed to work within the UK, although occasional trips abroad will not prevent it being UK employment.

The statutory scheme applies to all employment. Although there is machinery in the Whitley scheme for the review of disciplinary decisions including dismissals, the statutory rights are also fully available.

Entitlement to Claim

The employee must normally have two years continuous employment at the effective date of termination of the employment. This will normally be the date when any notice given expired. In order to avoid abuses an employee who is summarily dismissed can add on the statutory minimum period of notice applicable. This really only helps employees summarily dismissed in the week before they achieve two years service, as they are then deemed to have crossed the hurdle.

This qualification period does not apply to certain categories of unfair dismissal associated with trade union activities and membership.

There are special rules for certain part-time employees (*see Chapter 1*).

The employee must not have passed the normal retiring age for the employment. This may be specified in the contract or, if not, may be established by examining what occurs in practice. In the absence of such indications, or if these are discriminatory between men and women, the upper age limit will be 65.

Dismissal

Three situations are recognised as dismissal. The first is where the employer terminates an open-ended contract of employment, with or without notice. The second is where a fixed-term contract expires and is not renewed by the employer. The third is what is known as a 'constructive dismissal,' and occurs where the employee terminates the employment as a direct result of the employer's conduct, which must be serious enough to entitle the employee to leave without notice. The employee must not merely show that the employer has behaved badly, but that there has been a material breach of contract, such as an attempt to enforce geographical mobility not specified in the contract, or a breach of the duty of basic human respect.

Unfair Dismissal

An employee under a fixed-term contract for over a year can formally abandon the right to claim unfair dismissal on non-renewal of the contract.

Where dismissal is disputed it is for the employee to prove it has occurred. Normally if the employee resigns there is no dismissal; constructive dismissal provides an exception to this rule, and it is also possible to prove that an apparent resignation is void because it was given under duress. The mere threat of disciplinary proceedings may not amount to duress for these purposes. If however the employer has put matters clearly to the employee in terms of 'Resign or be Sacked,' this will almost certainly amount to duress.

The Reason for the Dismissal

Once the fact of dismissal has been established the employer must show what the reason or main reason for it was. The first step is to seek to show that it was for one of the permissible statutory reasons. If no reason is shown, or the reason is not one of the statutory ones, the dismissal will be unfair. If the reason is a statutory one the Industrial Tribunal decides whether the employer acted reasonably in dismissing. The statutory reasons are:

1. The capability or qualifications of the employee

Any initial problem of the competence of a new employee can of course be dealt with before they acquire rights under the legislation, as can the absence of claimed formal qualifications. There are a number of common problems.

Basic competence will usually only be an issue after a promotion or change of job. Appropriate training and support must have been given at the outset, and the employee must have been advised that their performance is inadequate. Such advice is loosely described as a warning, but it should not be confused with a disciplinary warning. If the problem is failure to master a promoted post, a retransfer to the old post may be an alternative to dismissal.

Decline in performance by an employee previously accepted as competent may stem from a variety of causes, ill-health, dissatisfaction etc. If it is a matter of attitude it becomes more a disciplinary issue. If the problem is an isolated example of negligence it will usually merit a warning unless the negligence is life-threatening. In this case the serious consequences may justify more drastic action. It is probably the case that to justify dismissal the negligence must be more than momentary inattention, or a slip of the hand, but it is hard to lay down hard and fast rules. The employer need only show a genuine and reasonable belief in the incompetence or negligence.

Long-term absence through ill-health clearly means the employee is incapable of doing the job. Whether it is reasonable to dismiss will depend on the prognosis, the length of employment and the nature of the job. As in the case of frustration a balancing exercise must be done. It will however usually be unreasonable to dismiss during a period of contractual paid sick leave.

Repeated minor illness may justify the issue of warnings. The system of self-certification is open to abuse. Reasonableness will again be judged in the light of the cumulative disruption to the operations of the employer.

There have been very few dismissals for **want of formal qualifications**, no doubt because these are usually obtained before applying for the job. If a trainee fails to achieve the final qualification, this would justify dismissal, at least after a reasonable opportunity to resit. Disqualification from driving will justify the dismissal of an employee whose job requires them to drive, such as a community nurse or health visitor. Loss of an essential professional qualification (e.g. striking off by the UKCC) would also justify dismissal.

2. The Conduct of the Employee

The categories of misconduct are infinite. To justify dismissal however the misconduct must make the employee unfitted to continue in employment, i.e. it must reflect on their suitability as an employee, not just on their general moral character. Relevant misconduct can be sub-divided into professional, industrial and non-work.

Professional misconduct is largely self-explanatory, e.g. abuse of drugs, deliberate or reckless neglect of patients and physical or sexual abuse of patients. All these matters may also be the subject of disciplinary proceedings by the UKCC.

Industrial misconduct is the sort of behaviour at work which is unacceptable on the part of any employee, e.g dishonesty, wilful damage to property, violence or drunkenness on duty, incivility, insubordination and absenteeism.

Non-work misconduct is a residual category of behaviour which, while occurring outside the work context nevertheless reflects on the employee as such. Convictions for homosexual acts have fallen into this category where the employee is working with the young and vulnerable.

Much attention has centred on the investigation of alleged misconduct. In general terms the obligation on the employer is to carry out an adequate investigation of the circumstances. This investigation covers two main areas: responsibility for the misconduct; and any explanation or mitigation which may be put forward. Many cases are purely internal and in such cases it is the responsibility of the employer to conduct such enquiries as are necessary to establish the facts and to consider the employee's representations about the matter. In many cases, the facts are clear, and are either admitted to the employee or are not in serious dispute. In such cases, the main function of the investigation is to establish any excuse or explanation. In other cases there may be a denial that there has been any misconduct, or that the suspected employee is to blame for something

Unfair Dismissal

which has occurred, but where responsibility is in doubt. In such cases, while it is recognised that the employer is conducting neither a police enquiry nor a court hearing, there is a duty to act with basic fairness and efficiency. If an external investigative agency—such as the police—is involved, it is not essential for the employer to wait until their enquiries and any subsequent prosecution have been completed before taking any disciplinary action. In such circumstances, it is not necessary for the employer to prove that the employee is guilty, merely that there were reasonable grounds for believing that she was. It is an essential ingredient in this enquiry that the employee be given an adequate explanation of what is alleged, the opportunity to deny the allegation and present a case if appropriate, and the opportunity to explain the position and make any excuse or put forward a claim for leniency. The model ACAS code of conduct allows for representation by a friend or Union official on these occasions, and the same will apply to Health Authority disciplinary rules under the Whitley arrangements. It used to be thought that there were some cases which were so clear and so serious that it was unnecessary to hear the employee, but it is now settled that the procedural aspect of fairness is essential, and therefore a failure to afford an opportunity of explanation will make the dismissal at least technically unfair. To sum up, then, the employer must be in a position to show:

- that the person actually making the decision to dismiss actually believed that the employer was guilty of the relevant misconduct;
- that this belief was reached on reasonable grounds and following an appropriate enquiry; and
- that dismissal was a reasonable penalty in the light of all the circumstances, including any excuse or mitigating factors.

3. Redundancy

The concept of redundancy is considered in Chapter 2. If the reason for dismissal is a bona fide redundancy, then it will not be unfair. It does not follow that every dismissal which is attributed to redundancy by the employer is in fact for that reason. Furthermore, even if there is a genuine redundancy situation, a particular dismissal may still be unfair. There may be selection otherwise than in accordance with the agreed procedure, or an absence of consultation.

4. Illegality of Continued Employment

This reason is rare. It can only arise if there are rules regulating who may do a job. Certain occupations are not open to pregnant women, but dismissal would only be justifiable if the woman could not be redeployed to a safe task.

5. Some other Substantial Reason (SOSR)

Employers and their operations vary enormously. It is impossible to lay down an exhaustive set of criteria for acceptable reasons for dismissal. SOSR is designed to allow the necessary flexibility, and therefore defies comprehensive definition. It certainly covers reorganisations of work activities which fall outside the strict definition of redundancy, and specifically includes dismissals for economic, technical or organisational reasons associated with the transfer of a business from one owner to another.

The Fairness of the Dismissal

In discussing the permissible statutory reasons comment has been made that in some situations dismissal may not be the only option. Once it has been established that the reason for the dismissal is a permissible one it is for the Industrial Tribunal to decide whether the dismissal was fair or unfair having regard to '*equity and the substantial merits of the case*'. The Tribunal will take account of the size and resources of the employer, and consider the matter in two stages; firstly was a proper procedure followed, and secondly did the decision on the merits fall within the '*band of reasonableness*'.

Employers should have a formal disciplinary procedure and this should be applied rigorously. Most are based on the code of practice issued by the Arbitration Conciliation and Advisory Service (ACAS). If there is no procedure, or it is not followed, it is highly likely that the dismissal will be held to be unfair. Some latitude is given to small employers, who will not be expected to have formal procedures laid down, but the employee must still be given a fair hearing.

The procedure to be adopted in cases which are not disciplinary in nature is less clear. There must be a full enquiry and consultation; the Tribunal is more concerned with the substance than the form of such enquiry, but this will not excuse a failure to use established procedures.

In some cases employers seek to argue that there was no need to hold any enquiry because there was a blatant case of gross misconduct, or a clear redundancy situation with no alternative course of action. This argument is usually rejected. it may well be that the employee could not have put anything forward to alter the decision, but she is entitled to the opportunity.

The concept of the '*band of reasonableness*' reflects the fact that there may be more than one acceptable response to a situation. If this is so, it is enough that the actual decision to dismiss was one of them. The Tribunal does not consider what decision it would have made on the facts, it merely reviews and declares acceptable or unacceptable the decision of the employer.

The Tribunal may decide that, although the dismissal was unfair, the employee has contributed to it. This would occur where the Tribunal considered dismissal an unreasonably harsh punishment for a piece of misconduct, but accepted that the employee was to a degree at fault. The effect of such a finding is to reduce the amount of compensation proportionately with the degree of fault. if the only basis for the finding of unfairness is procedural then the contribution, which is considered on the merits, may be 100%.

The employer can only rely on facts known to him at the time to justify his decision. After-acquired knowledge cannot logically have influenced the decision.

Remedies

The original intention was that those unfairly dismissed should normally be reinstated in their old job or, if that was impracticable, reengaged in a new one. Continuity of employment would be retained and there would be compensation for financial loss in the mean-time. The problem is that, leaving aside the fact that the original dismissal probably means that there has been a breakdown of the relationship, the protracted and often bitter Industrial Tribunal proceedings will often lead to bitter recrimination . For this reason relatively few complainants seek reinstatement. Even where it is sought it will not usually be ordered unless the employer appears willing to accept it.

The usual remedy is therefore monetary compensation. This comprises two elements, a basic award calculated broadly as a redundancy payment would be (and against which any redundancy payment already made can be set), and a compensatory award, in respect of loss of earnings and other remuneration. If the applicant is still unemployed the award can cover future loss, and it can also cover a shortfall between earnings in the old employment and the new. No award will be made for any period when the Tribunal consider that the applicant could have obtained employment if she had tried. There is a relatively low overall limit, so the maximum award represents between six and twelve months earnings.

All awards are subject to clawback in favour of the DSS of any unemployment benefit etc. paid, and may be reduced proportionately where there is a finding of contributory fault.

There are additional powers to award compensation beyond the normal statutory maximum but these only apply where an employer has refused to comply with an order for reinstatement and in certain claims arising out of membership or non-membership of trade unions.

Chapter 4:
Sexual and Racial Discrimination

The General Picture

Until relatively recently an employer could please himself who he employed or did not employ and how, short of dismissal, he treated his employees. This led to complaints that women and members of ethnic minorities were being unfairly treated, and as a result legislation was introduced to combat this. There are three specific statutes, the Race Relations Act, Sex Discrimination Act and Equal Pay Act. They form a single body of law, sharing many of the same concepts and with a common terminology. There are however significant differences. Racial discrimination is to be found in many non-employment contexts, and much of the Act is devoted to these. This is only true to a limited extent of sexual discrimination. The equal pay legislation is derived in part from provisions of European Community law which automatically applies in the UK and a number of decisions of the European Court of Justice have assisted in the interpretation and application of its provisions. There are also specific provisions relating to pregnancy and maternity; although not formally part of the same group of provisions, there is obviously some overlap between sex discrimination and pregnancy and maternity rights.

Because this area of law is of such recent origin it is still developing and the attitudes of those affected are still being shaped.

Common Concepts

The Race Relations Act and Sex Discrimination Act deal with three types of behaviour, direct discrimination, indirect discrimination and victimisation. It is in most cases irrelevant whether discrimination is deliberate or accidental; the law looks at the effect of behaviour rather than the motives of the person concerned. To a very limited extent the law will overlook trivial and accidental discrimination, as in the case where the complaint of male employees that they were discriminated against because their female colleagues were allowed to leave work five minutes early to beat the rush was rejected on the ground of triviality.

Discrimination in the field of employment may occur at any stage. It has been met with in relation to recruitment, in relation to job advertisements, general policies and specific appointments, access to promotion and training and termination of employment (selection for redundancy etc).

Direct Discrimination

This occurs when a person is treated less favourably than another on the relevant ground. It was held in a decided case to be direct discrimination for a nursing school to refuse a place on a course to a married woman with children who was otherwise qualified, on the ground that her possible need to care for her, school age, children might interfere with her attendance, while a male applicant with pre-school age children was not even questioned about his responsibilities to them, it being assumed that his partner was responsible. The woman had clearly been treated less favourably than the man. This case demonstrates that direct discrimination need not involve overt and intentional racism or sexism as the case may be; it is nevertheless true that most cases of direct discrimination are deliberate. Cases of direct discrimination may involve single individuals, as in disputes over specific appointments, or a group or class of people.

One area of particular difficulty is in appointments. If there is no formal shortlisting and interview procedure it may be difficult to establish who has applied, what their qualifications are and what criteria are applied by the appointor. Even where there is a formal procedure, the shortlisted candidates will all be regarded as suitable; it will be difficult to demonstrate that the public, non-discriminatory, reason given for the appointment, if indeed any reason is given, is a pretext or sham to hide the discriminatory truth. Occasionally the cat will be let out of the bag, but in a number of cases the only way to establish discrimination is to analyse applications and appointments over a period, consider the representation of the affected group in the particular workforce and in the population generally, and treat a significant disparity as evidence of malpractice. However research done in the 1980s into the under-representation of certain ethnic minority groups within the NHS found that this was largely because members of these groups did not apply for NHS jobs. Their under-representation was therefore due to their own choices rather than any current discrimination on the part of the NHS. The report did not seek to establish why these choices were being made, and it is at least possible that there was discrimination earlier which has had the effect of deterring applications over a substantial period of time.

Indirect Discrimination

This occurs when rules or conditions are applied evenly across the board to all comers. It will thus usually occur in relation to an organisation or occupational group as a whole. Since the rules apply to all equally there is no apparent or direct discrimination, there will however be indirect discrimination if it can be shown that the rules apply differentially to the disadvantaged group, in the sense either that a significantly smaller proportion of the group can comply with the condition, or that the rules apply to a disproportionately large number of that group, and, in either

Discrimination

case, it will be unlawful discrimination if the rule or condition in question cannot be objectively justified.

Under the first category it has been held that an insistence on UK educational qualifications is indirectly racially discriminatory, as a disproportionately large number of the ethnic minority community received their education abroad. While it would be objectively justifiable to require an appropriate level of education, equivalent overseas qualifications should be recognised, and the rule is therefore unlawful. Similarly a Civil Service age limit of 28 for entry to a grade of posts was held to be unlawfully indirectly discriminatory against women, since a disproportionately large proportion of them would be unable to apply in their twenties because of child care responsibilities. There was no objectively justifiable reason for this age limit.

In a very recent decision the High Court has ruled that the provisions of the employment legislation that provide less favourable treatment for part-time employees in respect of qualifying periods of continuous service (*see Chapter 1*) indirectly discriminate against women because they constitute the majority of part time workers, but that the provisions are not unlawful because they are objectively justified in that extending the rights of part-timers would lead to a reduction of part-time jobs.

Victimisation

This is a provision designed to ensure that there are no reprisals against those who take action to assert their primary rights under the discrimination provisions and those who assist them by providing or giving evidence in support of their case.

Racial Discrimination

The discrimination must be on racial grounds, which means 'colour, race, nationality or ethnic or national origins.' An ethnic group protected by virtue of its common ethnic origin must show a long shared history and cultural tradition. The Sikhs and Jews qualify, as they have a common geographical origin, language literature and religion, together with an identity as a separate group within a larger community, but Rastafarians do not, since in their case there is not a sufficiently long-established history. Discrimination purely on grounds of religion is not covered. There are certain exemptions from the provisions of the Act. The most important in the employment field is that which allows selection on racial grounds for a post where the duties involve the provision of personal services promoting the welfare of a defined racial group where these are most effectively provided by a member of that group. This would permit a health authority for example to employ a Bangladeshi community nurse to work in an area with a large Bangladeshi population, providing her work was concentrated within that group, on the basis that Bangladeshi women in particular are more likely to respond favourably to a nurse from their own community who speaks their language and understands the constraints of their culture.

Sex Discrimination

The legislation governs discrimination on grounds of sex or marital status. in other words the employer must treat men and women equally, and must also treat married and single people of either sex equally. This means that certain long standing assumptions, e.g. that men's employment is more important as they are the breadwinners, or that a married woman, or indeed any woman of child-bearing age, is a less eligible employee because she may leave or interrupt employment to have children, are no longer legitimate bases for decision making. The legislation does not cover discrimination on the ground of sexual orientation.

Sexual harassment may amount to unlawful discrimination. This will be so if the harasser is a sufficiently senior individual as to represent the employer, or where management are informed of harassment by junior colleagues but fail to take effective action in respect of these complaints.

It is lawful to discriminate where there is a genuine occupational requirement that the job be done by a person of one sex or the other. Such cases are rare.

Remedies for Discrimination

There are statutory bodies established to coordinate the elimination of both forms of discrimination (The Commission for Racial Equality and the Equal Opportunities Commission respectively). They have the resources to carry out general investigations, and are empowered to bring legal proceedings in their own right or to support action by individuals.

Individual Remedies

Where the discrimination arises in the employment field, complaint is made to an Industrial Tribunal. There is no qualifying period of employment. The Tribunal can make a declaration as to the legal position. It can also award compensation, including an amount for injury to feelings as well as any actual loss, and make recommendations as to future practice.

Collective Remedies

The two Commissions have power to carry out investigations, commission research and otherwise identify areas of discrimination. They may then issue formal non-discrimination notices addressed to employers requiring them to eliminate unacceptable practices. They also issue Codes of Practice, which have the same status as the ACAS codes, i.e. they are not legally binding but are strong evidence of good practice.

Discrimination

Equal pay

Article 119 of the Treaty of Rome establishing the EEC provides that '*each member State shall ... ensure and subsequently maintain the application of the principle that men and women should receive equal pay for equal work.*' Like many other provisions of the Treaty this one is deceptively simple. The article itself confirms that pay includes all forms of remuneration and subsequent cases have confirmed that it covers fringe benefits of all kinds and pension rights. Equal means not only 'the same as' but also 'of equal value to'; the definition of these terms and the exploration of their ramifications has provided many thousands of hours of harmless fun and enjoyment for lawyers throughout the Community. While most of the important questions appear to have been settled with some degree of finality there are still constant developments. The Equal Pay Act itself predates our entry into the EEC, but has now been amended to take account of Article 119 and also more detailed rules issued by the EEC. Although most of the cases concern claims by women to equality of treatment with higher paid men, the Article and the Act also work in the reverse direction. The Act also covers self-employed people personally carrying out duties under a contract for services.

The Equality Clause

This clause is implied into every contract of employment and provides that whenever the employee is doing equal work (as defined in the Act) with a member of the opposite sex any term of the contract which is less favourable than that of the other is to be amended to be the same, and any benefit conferred on the other shall be conferred on the applicant. In other words it provides a mechanism for ensuring equal remuneration for equal work.

Equal Work

The statutory definition recognises three distinct situations where work will be equal:
- **Like work** is work that is essentially the same. The duties need not be identical, but they must be similar and make similar demands.
- If the employer has carried out a **formal job evaluation** scheme, jobs which are equally rated will be equal work. The job evaluation scheme must have been properly designed and carried out. If it is itself discriminatory in that it fails to give proper weight to all relevant factors it will be invalid.
- The third category is the one that has caused virtually all the problems. This is the category of **work of equal value**. Any woman can assert that her job is of equal value to the job of any

man employed by the same employer (the comparator). This is so even if the woman is working alongside a man engaged on like work who is paid equally with her. The work of the comparator need not be similar to that of the woman. Where an equal value claim is made to the Industrial Tribunal, and a preliminary review shows that it is not hopelessly misconceived, the Tribunal will order a formal job evaluation. If that evaluation upholds the equal value claim, the woman will prima facie be entitled to equal pay. There are however various facts which will justify pay differentials in equal value cases, although it is for the employer to prove that they apply. In working out whether the woman is receiving equal pay, each provision of the contract is taken separately. If the woman's basic pay is lower she is entitled to have it raised. The employer cannot set higher fringe benefits against lower basic pay, or claim to have the whole remuneration package looked at unless he can prove that there are separate and distinct categories of employees with their own separately negotiated terms and conditions (e.g. Works employees and Staff employees) and the woman and the comparator fall into different groups.

Factors justifying Differentials

A differential in pay will be justified if it is based on a genuine material factor (GMF) which distinguishes the two cases. Some GMFs are applicable in all cases, others only to equal value cases.

The generally applicable GMFs, which must of course themselves operate evenhandedly as between the sexes are:

- A difference in the time when or the place where the work is done, such as an unsocial hours payment or a London weighting allowance.
- An objectively established skill or performance premium.
- A pay scale with increments for age, length of service and relevant qualifications or prior experience.
- 'Red circling,' where an employee is not being paid the rate for the job but is continuing to receive a higher rate for a previous job from which he has been redeployed.

In equal value cases the employer can claim economic factors as a GMF. This means that a scarcity premium may be justified.

Discrimination

Pensions

The equal pay legislation does not affect the differential state pensionable age. This is specifically left as a matter for national governments by the Treaty of Rome, and indeed there is a very substantial diversity of pensionable ages within the EEC.

Until the retirement age was fixed at 65 for both sexes there were a number of cases in which women successfully claimed that enforced early retirement indirectly deprived them of access to equal pay. These cases are now of historic interest only.

Until recently it was believed that occupational pension schemes were outside the scope of the equal pay legislation, and could therefore make differential provision. It has now been decided that they are within the scope, but in view of the serious consequences on the pension funds of requiring them to pay pensions on a vastly different basis to that on which the rates of contribution and benefit were calculated, the decision only operates prospectively and does not allow prior dealings to be reopened. An EC ruling was made at the Maastricht conference in December 1991 that the ruling will in fact only apply to service from 1991. Pension providers are at the time of writing still engaged in settling the detailed revised rules of their various schemes.

Pregnancy

Dismissal of a woman because she is pregnant or for a reason connected with the pregnancy will be unfair, unless the woman has also become unfit to work, or normally works with radioactive materials or teratogenic chemicals and cannot be redeployed. It is an unfair selection for redundancy to select a woman because she is pregnant, but if she is a natural candidate for selection on the basis of the agreed procedure the fact of the pregnancy will not protect her. The usual two year qualifying period will apply. A woman without the qualifying period may be able to show sexual discrimination, but there are logical difficulties, since it is impossible to establish how the employer would treat a pregnant man, although the Tribunal may accept the analogy of a disease which would have the same sort of impact on attendance at work.

Maternity

Many employers, including the NHS, operate contractual maternity pay and maternity leave schemes. Each has its own detailed rules and procedures. In addition there is a statutory scheme.

Statutory Maternity Pay (SMP)

The scheme operates in the same way as statutory sick pay (SSP), i.e. it is paid by the employer on behalf of the state. Where there is a contractual scheme the SMP will simply form part of the payments made by the employer. The entitlement depends on the woman having achieved a period of continuous service prior to 14 weeks before her expected week of confinement (EWC) and on her earnings over the eight weeks preceding that date averaging at least the lower earnings limit for National Insurance Contributions.

If she has over two years continuous employment she is entitled to six weeks SMP at a rate equal to 90% of her average pay, which she may take at any time within the period six weeks before to seven weeks after the EWC, together with a further 12 weeks SMP at a lower rate equal to the lower rate of SSP for the time being to be taken within the period 11 weeks before to 11 weeks after the EWC.

If she has over six months continuous service she is entitled to 18 weeks SMP at the lower rate during the period of 11 weeks before to 11 weeks after the EWC.

If she has less than six months continuous service there is no right to SMP but there is an entitlement to DSS maternity allowance.

Statutory Maternity Leave

This is a complex scheme. there are many rigid time limits and notice provisions; if these are not adhered to rights under the scheme may be lost, and it is therefore essential for any woman who intends to rely on the scheme to get the necessary documentation from the DSS in advance and to ensure she follows the prescribed timetable scrupulously. The intention of the legislation is to give an entitlement to a total of approximately 40 weeks maternity leave (the precise amount depends on whether the birth takes place on schedule). This is however achieved in a rather roundabout way by actually giving the woman a right to return after giving birth subject to fulfilling various conditions.

The woman must have two years continuous service immediately prior to the eleventh week before the EWC. While she must actually still be in employment at that time she need not be actually working. She may be on holiday or on sick leave. If she has resigned with effect earlier than that date she has irrevocably abandoned her statutory rights.

She must give at least three weeks notice stating:

- that she intends to be absent by reason of pregnancy or confinement;
- that she intends to return to work;
- what is the EWC.

The notice is not a binding commitment, and is usually given whatever the woman's actual intentions, so as to cover all eventualities. It cannot however be informally withdrawn. There are special rules to cover premature births.

Discrimination

Seven weeks after the EWC the employer may request the woman to confirm within two weeks whether she intends to return. If she fails to give this confirmation she will normally lose the right to return.

The return to work must be within 29 weeks of the actual birth, and the woman must give three weeks notice of the return date. She may return earlier if she wishes. Once a return date has been set, the employer may defer actual return for up to four weeks for operational reasons and the woman may do so for health reasons.

Where the woman has complied with her procedural obligations but the employer refuses to allow her to return this is deemed to be a dismissal on the date of the refusal. If the employer employs five people or less the dismissal will be fair if he cannot reasonably practicably provide her with work. In other cases the dismissal will be unfair unless it is due to redundancy or the woman has unreasonably refused an alternative post.

The Whitley Scheme

This scheme, which is set out in Section 6 of the General Agreement, is modelled closely in many respects on the general statutory scheme. It does, however, provide that certain breaks in service will not break continuity. In addition, only twelve months' full-time service is required to qualify for maternity leave with pay, and the notification requirements are somewhat simpler. There is provision for 18 weeks maternity leave without pay when the woman has less than 12 months service, or is a part-timer. A woman with 12 months service who intends to return to work is entitled to 8 weeks' full pay (less SMP or other benefits received or deemed to be received where a married woman is paying reduced NI contributions), plus 10 weeks at half pay (less benefits) and to a total of 52 weeks' maternity leave in total. One who does not intend to return is entitled to 6 weeks' pay at $9/10ths$ of the full rate, provided she has completed two years full-time or equivalent service, or five years part-time service. The minimum weekly hours are, as usual, 16 and 8, respectively.

The General Whitely Council has urged authorities to develop retainer schemes (Section 50, General Agreement) which allows employees away from work for an extended period (among other causes) child rearing, to retain a link with the employer, with a view to maintaining skills and facilitating return. A period on retainer will preserve continuity of employment, although it does not itself constitute employment.

Exercises

1   Distinguish between direct and indirect discrimination.

2.   What would be your course(s) of action if you met a case of:
    a) sexual discrimination;
    b) racial discrimination;
    c) pay discrimination?

Employment Law

Which regulations govern action in these three areas?

3. If a nurse wishes to have a baby and return to work, what are her entitlements under NHS rules? How should she ensure that she is eligible for these entitlements?

Chapter 5:
The National Health Service

The General Whitley Council

This is the principal national negotiating body within the NHS. It determines the NHS redundancy scheme. This operates to the exclusion of the normal statutory scheme. Certain other statutory rights are also excluded because the existence of the Whitley machinery covers the ground. The General Council also deals with the grievance and disciplinary procedures and employee relations generally.

The grievance procedure is set out in Section 32. It provides that after a hearing by the employing authority as the final stage in their local internal grievance procedure, there is a right of recourse to a Regional Appeals Committee, comprised of members of the management and staff sides of the General Council. The right of appeal is vested in the relevant trade union or staff association, and the purpose of the procedure is to resolve matters of general concern, not purely personal problems.

The general guidelines for disciplinary proceedings take the form of a procedural framework laying down how proceedings are to be conducted. It is for the individual authority to establish its own rules defining disciplinary offences and penalties.

Provisions has also been made recently to ensure that whistle blowers are not penalised by inappropriate disciplinary action. It remains to be seen whether these provisions are effective. Generally, the fate of the whistle blower has been an unhappy one.

Most of the rest of the general agreement is taken up with detailed provisions relating to leave of absence in a variety of special situations, in particular public duties of many kinds. There are also detailed provisions on travel and other expenses.

Pay Bargaining

The forum for this was originally the Nurses and Midwives Whitley Council (NMWC), but the function is now exercised by the Review Body for Nursing Staff, Midwives, Health Visitors and Professions Allied to Medicine (the Review Body). The NMWC is restricted to making submissions to the Review Body. The Review Body receives evidence from the interested parties and submits a report to the Health Secretary. Although the primary concern of the Review Body is salary levels, it can and does address other issues related to terms and conditions of service. It was for example instrumental in initiating the clinical regrading exercise. The Health Secretary can either accept or reject the report, but acceptance does not involve a commitment to fund the recommendations. The ultimate policy goal of the present government is to abolish national salary structures, even for those employees who remain employed by regional district or special health authorities. Local bargaining will take economic factors such as scarcity into account.

The Contract of Employment

This is drawn up by the employing authority, although it will contain the national terms and conditions of the General Council and will incorporate salary structures based on the current Review Body scales, as implemented by the Government. It will also incorporate any general policies and procedures of the employing authority on such matters as discipline, equal opportunities grievances etc. All these matters are normally incorporated by reference, and the actual documents are made available for consultation. The specific details of the post will be set out, together with a flexibility clause which will allow the authority considerable latitude in the deployment of staff, subject to a requirement of reasonableness in relation to changes to established work patterns.

As has been pointed out, each authority draws up its own disciplinary rules; in practice there is considerable overlap between these. Typically they will spell out the suspect's rights to representation by a colleague or trade union official, lay down rules for the conduct of investigations, define what conduct is classed as ordinary and which as gross misconduct and the range of available penalties, and provide for an internal appeal. The procedural rules will be taken from section 40 of the General Whitley Council Agreement. It is now normal for unauthorised disclosure of information relating to individual patients or to the activities of the authority to be classed as misconduct.

It is not unfair to say that the procedures so established are formal and complex. There is a slight advantage to an employee in this respect, since it will not be an attractive option for the management to implement these procedures unless there is a serious issue. It may therefore be the case that minor disagreements are resolved by informal means; these will be less stressful for the employee, since there is no possibility of action being taken to terminate employment. disciplinary powers are reserved to senior officers of the authority and there is a right of appeal to a committee of the authority. Grievance procedures are also formal, and the same observations apply. In this case the formality of the procedure may work against the interests of the employee, in that she will not seek to implement these procedures unless there is no alternative, but informal channels of complaint may not produce effective redress.

Rider to Contract of Employment

The document produced for any nurse is therefore a very complex one. It must always be remembered firstly that the operation of national review mechanisms will affect the detailed provisions, and also that the transfer of a the majority of NHS activities to trusts will mean that the national conditions will progressively cease to apply. At present, the following aspects of the contract are regulated by the Nursing and Midwifery Staffs Negotiating Council.

- **Annual leave**, which for qualified nurses and midwives and third- and fourth-year students is five weeks plus public and statutory holidays.
- **Sick leave and sick pay**. There is no definition of the maximum sick leave, but there is a definition of the maximum period for which there is an entitlement to sick pay. This varies with the length of service, rising from one month on full pay in the first year:

First year of service	One month's full pay (plus two months on half pay after completing two months' service)
Second year of service	Two months' full and two months' half pay
Third year of service	Four months' full and four months' half pay
Fourth/fifth year of service	Five months' full and five months' half pay
Thereafter	Six months' full and six months' half pay

These periods will be extended on a discretionary basis. the payments will incorporate statutory sick pay where due. The rules apply top part-timers with full and half pay defined by reference to their actual pay during the preceding period.

- **Pay adjustments on transfers**. In essence an nurse who is transferred at her own request or because of incompetence or unsuitability has no protection of her salary and status, but other nurses who are transferred, or whose post is downgraded, have their salary safeguarded. If necessary, they will mark time until the salary scale for the new post catches up. The detailed rules are necessarily complex, and should be studied with the aid of a qualified helper in each particular case.

Employment Law

Exercises

1. What is the grievance procedure for NHS employees under the Whitley Council rules?
2. What aspects of nurses' employment are governed by the Whitley Council rather than Statutory rules?

Chapter 6:
NHS Trusts

The National Health Service and Community Care Act 1990 made provision for the establishment of NHS Trusts. These trusts would take over the ownership and management of hospitals and other establishments and facilities previously managed by health authorities as a part of the NHS, or could provide and manage new facilities for health care. The first such trusts are now in operation and the intention of the present government is to extend the number of trusts so that the majority of hospitals and other providers of health care within the NHS are operating within a trust. The principle is that the District Health Authorities should largely cease to be providers of health care, and should concentrate on procuring health care on behalf of their clients, the population of the district. This role will, in fact, be shared with those GPs who have become fund-holders. They are responsible for negotiating arrangements for the treatment of their patients by local hospitals and community care organisations, whether trusts or units still directly managed by the district health authority. The staff employed by the relevant health authority at the relevant establishments were transferred to the employment of the trust when it commenced operations, and in the event of further trusts being established, the same procedure will be followed. The Act lays down the terms of transfer and also makes provision for those employed partly for the purposes of a trust and partly for the purposes of the original authority.

Full transfer

In the case of employees employed solely at or for the purposes of the establishment transferred to the NHS Trust, their contract of employment will be treated as though it was made between the employee and the Trust, in substitution for the authority as from the operational date of the trust. Similar provisions apply to employees of the authority who transfer to the Trust in the setting up period before the operational date. It is expressly declared that all the authority's rights, powers, duties and liabilities under the contract are transferred to the Trust. This in effect means that the employee retains continuity of employment with the actual seniority they have acquired. The initial terms and conditions of employment with the trust will be the current terms and conditions of the authority. As such they will incorporate the Whitley Council contractual redundancy scheme, and all the policies and procedures contained or referred to in the contract itself.

The Trust is outside both the Whitley and Review Body machinery, and it is open to the management of the Trust to introduce revised terms and conditions to the extent that they see fit. In practice salaries within Trusts may be expected to remain in line with those paid by authorities to their remaining staff, but this will be as the result of the operation of economic market forces and not as a result of any legal obligation. Equally it will be open to Trusts to modify other conditions. The Act expressly envisages that Trusts may abandon the contractual redundancy scheme. In this case employees would acquire a statutory entitlement, and the Act ensures that they can only recover the higher figure rather than claiming both. Over a period of time each Trust will therefore develop its own distinctive contract of employment. anyone considering taking employment with a Trust will need to consider the nature of these, just as employees of commercial companies do. It will not be possible to assume that the conditions are roughly the same as is the case under the traditional NHS system.

Employees with split responsibilities

The Act requires that the relevant authority should devise a scheme whereby in effect the contracts of such employees are split, and they end up employed by the Trust under a contract covering that part of their work which related to the Trust's facilities (and to which the general transfer rules stated above applies), and by the authority in respect of the rest of their work. as these will be part time contracts there is special provision made whereby for the purposes of continuity of employment the number of hours worked under either contract is deemed to be the number of hours worked under both together, and each is deemed to be a continuation of the original employment. It would however seem that this special protection only continues while the employee continues to work under both contracts. If the employee leaves one of the jobs, it seems the other reverts to ordinary part time status. It is not clear whether a change of job while still working for the same employer will have the same effect.

It can thus be seen that the employment implications of NHS Trusts are far from straightforward. The future of the Trust concept is still uncertain and dependent on political developments which cannot be predicted. If, however, Trusts are abolished by fresh legislation, or indeed if an individual Trust becomes unviable and is reabsorbed into the traditional NHS structure, there will be complex employment law considerations if the terms and conditions of its employees have in the meantime been altered from the Whitley norms.

Officially the transfer of facilities to trusts is designed to achieve greater efficiency as a result of managerial reform, and the effect on employees is neutral. In practice trusts are being encouraged by advice from unofficial think tanks with links to the members of the present government to consider a variety of approaches to staffing which depart radically from previous practice. Thus trusts are being encouraged to consider employing only a core staff on a permanent basis, and to use short fixed-term contracts or agency staff to meet other requirements on a short-term basis. It is also being suggested that certain tasks heretofore considered as requiring trained nursing staff, such as the care of the convalescent, can be entrusted to non-nursing staff, with qualified indirect supervision. While these measures are undoubtedly economically attractive to the managers of the trusts, they are less so to employees, who may be faced with less good terms and conditions, specifically in relation to security of employment, while the extended use of unskilled personnel may have implications for professional responsibility.

Changing the Terms

There is, as has been pointed out above, nothing in law to prevent the management of a trust seeking to change the terms and conditions of employment of a Trust employee once transfer has occurred. The whole rationale of establishing trusts is to give them the power to run their own activities as they see fit, and the establishment of 'appropriate' terms and conditions is an aspect of this. In the past, the whole of the NHS was a single system, and there was no need for one part of it to keep secrets from another part. Indeed, the whole ethos of healthcare was to publish or share information, whether of new medical or surgical discoveries, or of improvements in efficiency and operation of the system itself. In the present competitive environment, much information is seen as commercially sensitive and therefore confidential. This provides a justification for the introduction of new terms prohibiting employees from disclosing information relating to the Trust to outsiders. When applied to information of a financial or commercial nature: income, costings for various activities, bed occupancy etc., this requirement is justified, and merely mirrors normal practice in most sectors of commerce and industry. Such requirements have also been applied to information directly related to patient care and other professional matters. To this extent, such clauses create a conflict of interest of the kind discussed in Chapter 1. They are therefore objectionable, but as pointed out in Chapter 1, the law tends to respect such rights at the expense of the public interest in the dissemination of information.

Another change which is likely to be made is the abandonment of the nationally established NHS grades and salary scales. A single trust will of course be competing for staff with other health-care providers locally and nationally, so will not be able to step too far out of line, especially where there is no pool of unemployed available on less advantageous terms. The inevitable growth of a variety of sets of conditions will make the job of choosing whether to seek a post with particular Trust a difficult one. It may be that trusts will offer a different package, or menu of benefits to different employees. In some respects, this may be beneficial. A given trust may put a high priority on attracting working mothers, and therefore offer conditions (e.g. work rotas fitting in with school hours) or facilities such as

Employment Law

a creche or playgroup, which are particularly attractive to such women, while another may place the emphasis on recruiting and retaining full-time, career-oriented staff. The onus must be on the employing trust to make its policy clear in advertising and interviewing for posts, but also on the individual to ensure that she is seeking employment which meets her own needs. There is likely to be no remedy short of resigning and trying again elsewhere if a wrong decision is made.

Exercise

1. If the organisation employing you acquires Trust status, what effects may this have on your contract of employment?

Chapter 7:
Trade Unions

The Nature of Trade Unions

Trade Unions are independent, self-regulating voluntary associations of workers in a particular industry or area of activity, associated together by employment by the same employer, or by having the same trade or profession. Their principal purpose is to represent their membership for the purpose of negotiations with the employer in respect of pay and other terms and conditions of employment, usually referred to as collective bargaining. In addition to this Unions also provide individual assistance to their members in dealing with their managers in connection with individual grievances and disciplinary problems. Union officials will represent and negotiate on behalf of the member as appropriate. This assistance will usually also be available at internal disciplinary proceedings and also at Industrial Tribunals. Unions also provide legal advice and assistance to members, at all events in relation to legal problems arising out of employment, such as claims for compensation arising out of industrial accidents or disease. In some cases this extends also to legal problems in general. The membership fee includes insurance cover for claims against the member as a result of negligence at work. Unions also operate benevolent funds. Historically they provided a major source of sick pay, unemployment benefit, and pensions, but these functions have been largely taken over by the welfare state; many unions are however now offering a variety of financial services to members as a commercial venture. Most unions also take a very active interest in education and training.

The position of unions has been politically highly contentious for some years. Most unions are affiliated to the Labour party, although the unions and the party are distinct entities with their own policies and priorities. It has been a tenet of Conservative industrial policy that the activities of the unions have been harmful to the economy, and that the unions enjoyed excessive power which was exercised undemocratically. This has resulted in a number of Acts of Parliament intended to reform the unions. These reforms were, by and large, unwelcome to the unions and their leadership. Prior to these Acts of Parliament, unions had been almost entirely self-regulating, and they were certainly responsible for their own constitutions. Parliament has now prescribed how certain important functions are to be carried out, by requiring periodic election of the executive officers of the union, imposing ballots in a particular form before industrial action is taken, and by reinforcing the right not to belong to a union.

In theory, there should be one and only one union for each group of workers. this is not the case in practice. For historical reasons there may be two or more unions with members in a particular area. Thus both COHSE and NUPE have nurse members. In addition there are professional associations, which carry out many of the functions of unions in relation to individual and collective negotiations, as well as providing ancillary services, but which are not trade unions in the political sense. The RCN is in this category. In a number of cases the various unions and associations make common cause, but there are also situations where they take a different tactical position, or even, in extreme cases, disagree in principle.

One area of union activity which has always been controlled to some extent is that of political objects. These are activities which go beyond the improvement of the terms and conditions of employment of members. They thus bear on the organisation of society at large. A union may only pursue political objects if the members have voted to establish a political fund. This decision must be periodically confirmed. The political fund must be kept separate, and the general funds of the Union may not be used to support political activities. Individual members have the right not to contribute to the political fund.

Although there are close links between the trade union movement and the Labour party at both local and national level, not all political objects are party political. Many unions maintain a political fund even though they are not affiliated to the Labour party, because the definition of political objects is so wide that many areas of economic policy which are of obvious relevance to union members as such fall within the definition of 'political'. In a nursing context, it would be political in this sense for a union to become involved with issues related to the philosophy of health care delivery, the role of the private sector and other such matters. Although clearly of vital interest to nurses, these issues do not bear directly on terms and conditions of employment.

Historically, different unions had developed their own styles of self-organisation. Some were centralised, others devolved power to the branches; some gave ultimate control to full-time officers, others to a delegate council. The recent legislative changes have created greater uniformity, and one ground of objection was that the government was prescribing rules that forced unions to abandon traditional procedures which had stood the test of time. It is certainly now the case that all major decisions are taken by the membership as a whole, and therefore the pursuit of political objects is perfectly legitimate, as it will reflect the democratic wishes of the majority, not the sectional interests of activists, as was sometimes the case previously.

Union Membership

All employees have the right to join an independent trade union and participate in its activities at appropriate times. In other words, the employer cannot prevent his employees joining a union. Where an employee is dismissed for exercising these rights, the dismissal will be unfair; furthermore the usual two-year qualifying period will not apply. The employer is not obliged to allow union activities to take place in working hours in the case of ordinary members. The employee does not have a free choice of union. This is because the unions have an agreement regulating which areas they will operate in. There may be a choice if, as with COHSE and NUPE, two or more unions have members in the same area. It would of course be inconvenient and impractical for unions to recruit members from areas where they were not already active unless it was a previously non-unionised area.

Conversely an employee also has the right to refuse to join a union, or to resign from one, even if it is recognised by the employer, whether or not recognition involves a 'closed shop'. Dismissal for exercising these rights is automatically unfair. If it can be shown that the union has put pressure on the employer to dismiss, the union will be jointly responsible for paying compensation. In this case (although not where dismissal is for joining a union) there are special rules which increase the maximum awards of compensation substantially beyond the usual limits.

A member of a union is subject to the rules of the union; if those rules are broken, the union can discipline the member in default. While disciplinary proceedings are an internal matter, the courts have intervened where the procedures were themselves unfair, or were being operated unfairly or unreasonably. There is therefore a measure of control over the internal activities of unions in their dealings with their members.

The decision whether to join a union or a professional association, and if so, which of the available options to choose, is therefore essentially one for the individual to take in the light of her political and professional attitudes. Of course only members can influence union policy or take advantage of peripheral benefits, while all employees will be bound by the result of collective bargains struck between the unions and the employer. It is therefore sensible to join a Union which is recognised for collective bargaining purposes. Even when the Union is not recognised, the individual services in the field of insurance and legal assistance are valuable.

Collective Bargaining

As has been indicated above, one of the principal function of trade unions is to negotiate with employers in relation to terms and conditions, especially salaries. Within the NHS this was done through the national Whitley council machinery. It is now dealt with by the Review Body (*see Chapter 5*). Each NHS trust is now a separate employer, and unless they organise a consortium of employers, it will be necessary to negotiate separately with each, as has always been the case in the private sector. A distinctive feature of collective agreements is that they do not normally

Employment Law

represent legally binding contracts. The relevant terms are incorporated into the individual contracts of employment of the members and thus achieve legal effect. The parties to a collective agreement are free to decide that it will be legally binding, and there have been a number of legislative interventions which sought to make such agreements binding.

Industrial Action

Disagreements will occur between employers and employees from time to time. Where these disagreements affect the workforce generally, they will normally be represented by their Union. If it is clear that matters cannot be resolved by direct negotiations, there are two further possibilities.

The first is to refer the dispute to a third party to act as an arbitrator. Such arbitration can take a wide variety of forms. The arbitrator may be appointed on an *ad hoc* basis, or there may be an arbitration scheme contained in the agreement establishing the negotiating machinery. The parties may agree that the arbitrator's decision is to be final and binding, or it may merely be a recommendation. The arbitrator may be bound simply to find for one of the parties and against the other (so called 'pendulum arbitration'), or he may be at liberty to reach whatever conclusion he considers appropriate. The virtue of pendulum arbitration, especially in relation to pay claims, is that it compels both sides to be realistic. The arbitrator is bound to find for the proposal that is closest to his own assessment of what is right, and an unduly optimistic claim by the Union, or an unduly mean offer by the employer are likely to be too far from the arbitrator's position.

It certainly appears to be the case that agreements which incorporate arrangements for binding arbitration, often coupled with a 'no strike' clause, are becoming common.

The second option, which may be chosen instead of arbitration where there is no prior agreement to submit to arbitration, or which may follow a non-binding arbitrator's award which is not accepted, is recourse to industrial action. This phrase covers all the steps which employees can take to induce the employer to comply with their claims. It also covers steps taken by the employer for the same purpose, but it is uncommon today for an employer to do more than refuse to concede what the employees are demanding. It is usual to divide industrial action into strike action and industrial action short of strike action. There has been for many years an active debate as to the propriety of industrial action, or at least strike action, in areas such as health and education where any action, although aimed at the employer, directly affects the users of the service, patients and pupils. Some Unions as a result have a policy that they will not take strike action. In such areas the establishment of binding arbitration may be the best means of resolving the issue of the adverse effect of industrial action on innocent bystanders.

Industrial action can take a variety of forms:

Trade Unions

- **Strikes:** A strike is the withdrawal of labour by an employee in order to secure some advantage from the employer. Legally speaking there is no distinction between a short-term strike (e.g. for a day or half a day) and a long-term or indefinite strike. A strike is in law a repudiatory breach of contract by the employee. The employer is quite entitled to treat the employment as being at an end. No claim for unfair dismissal can be brought unless the employer is guilty of victimisation, in that he does not dismiss all strikers, or subsequently reinstates some but not all. It is uncommon for employers to sack strikers in this way, but it is not unknown. Usually the employer is keenly aware that he would need to recruit and train a set of replacements, and this may be impracticable or undesirable. It should however be borne in mind that there is a risk associated with striking. The temptation to dismiss strikers will be strongest when only a part of the relevant section of the work-force has joined the strike, or where the employer is trying to shed employees anyway.
- **Refusal to carry out full normal duties:** The employer is entitled to demand that the employee carries out all her duties. He is thus entitled to treat a refusal to carry out selected duties as a repudiation of the contract. If the employee is excluded from work for taking such action she is not entitled to be paid. Only where the employer clearly indicates that he accepts the situation will be liable to pay the employee for periods of restricted work, and even then he is entitled to make a deduction in respect of the work not done.
- **Overtime bans:** In some cases the employee's contract of employment requires her to work overtime. There is therefore a contractual obligation to do so, within the limits agreed. A refusal to work such contractual overtime is therefore a repudiatory breach of contract by the employee. The employer may treat it as grounds for dismissal, and if he does so the employee is not entitled to pursue a claim for unfair dismissal on the merits of the case. If there is no obligation to work overtime, a refusal to do so is entirely lawful, and however much the employer may be discommoded by this he will have no redress.
- **Work to Rule:** in theory an employer cannot complain if employees insist on working in strict accordance with the employer's own rules and regulations. In practice a work to rule amounts to an abuse of these rules in a deliberate attempt

to create difficulties for the employer. If it does take this form it will amount to a breach of the (express or implied) term in the employee's contract of employment to do what is reasonable to ensure the smooth running of the employer's business.

- **Work to Grade:** this is a relatively new concept. It presupposes that the employer has created a comprehensive grading system for posts, but that there are employees who are being required to do a job, the specification for which puts it in a higher grade than the one the employee is being paid under. The employee restricts herself to those duties which are within the competence of someone of her grade. It is thus a cross between a refusal to carry out full duties and a work to rule. The employee's duties to be flexible and professional mean that a request to take on a higher grade function for a short period (for example because of sickness or other temporary staff shortages) would be reasonable, and refusal would be unreasonable, unless the specific duties of the higher grade post were such that the employee would be putting herself or others at risk because she was not adequately trained or experienced. The employer is not entitled to require an employee to carry out duties on a long-term basis which he has himself confirmed are appropriate to a higher grade. On the other hand the employee is not entitled to interpret the requirements of a particular post too narrowly, or to refuse to carry out the duties traditionally associated with the post she holds simply because of the way these have been dealt with under the grading system.

It must be noted that where an employee is dismissed while taking industrial action no claim for unfair dismissal can be entertained unless there is victimisation (as discussed under Strikes above). There is no comprehensive definition of industrial action. It would seem that any action undertaken for the purpose of inducing the employer to concede demands of the employees will count, even if it does not amount to a breach of contract.

Exercises

1. What unions are open to those working in health care?
2. List the pros and cons of belonging to a trade union.

Final Exercise

Find out all you can about your contract of employment, and especially:

- Do you have a written contract of employment? (Express terms)
- Are there other unwritten terms usual for your type of employment? (Implied terms)
- Are details of some of the contract terms available in other documents (e.g. grievance procedure)? If so, where can these documents be consulted?
- Is your employer an NHS or an NHS Trust working under the normal Whitley Council machinery? If not, how do the terms and conditions of your employment vary from those of an NHS establishment?

Appendix:
Quick Guide:
Employment Law for Nurses

What should I know about my employment status?

- Are you employed or self-employed?
- Who is your employer (National Health Service, Trust, Agency, Self)?
- If you work for an Agency, what is your insurance position?
- Does you contract of employment contain a mobility clause?

See pp. 1, 3–6

What laws/statutes/rules are important?

- All employed people (in any sector) are subject to general employment law as laid down by Parliament and the Employment Protection (Consolidation) Act, Industrial Tribunals, Employment Appeals Tribunal, as well as to the specific rules of their employers (See Chapter 1).
- For employed nurses the specific rules of the employer (the NHS or NHS Trusts) are governed by the Whitley Council machinery. Modifications to the Whitley Council rules may be made by the NHS Trusts (See Chapter 6). There may be a variety of different rules in agencies and the private sector.
- Self-employed nurses are responsible for themselves in most respects and should consult rules for self-employed people in general (outside the scope of this book).
- All practising nurses (whatever their employment status) are subject to the rules of professional discipline established and administered by the UKCC.

In what areas do these laws/statutes/rules apply?

- UK Common Law
- Right to damages for wrongful dismissal
- UK Statutory Rights
- Compensation for redundancy (Chapter 2)
- Equality as regards sex and pay (Chapter 6)
- Maternity leave/pay (p 2, 37–39)
- Protection against unfair dismissal (Chapter 3)

Appendix:

- Sick pay
- Unemployment benefit
- European Community Law
- Equality of treatment on the grounds of sex
- The Whitley Council operates its own redundancy scheme (p 22), grievance and disciplinary procedures and generally governs employee relations in the nursing profession.

What should I be careful about when changing jobs?

Be alert to the professional content of the post **and also** the general employment policies of the employer.

- Tangible—Express terms (p. 11–12)
- Holiday entitlement
- Hours of work
- Job description
- Maternity leave
- Pay scales/rates
- Period of notice
- Place of employment
- Sick pay/leave
- Intangible—attitudes (p 2) of the employer towards:
- Time off for child rearing
- Job sharing

These may be explicit (i.e. set out in a written contract of employment) or implicit (matters which according to codes and practice, routinely apply to employment of this type). See p 6–8, 42–43, Chapter 6 for NHS Trusts). Even in the absence of a written statement, a contract of employment may be deemed to exist (p 8).

Agency nurses should be very clear on the insurance position (p.5–6)

What are the major areas where conflicts of interest arise?

Loyalty to employer vs. duty to patients ('whistle-blowing') (p.9, 12–13, 41)
- Striking, working to rule or grade vs. patient well-being (p. 10–11, 52–53)

Should I belong to a Union?

- See Chapter 7.

Index

A

ACAS Code of Practice, 28
Acts of Parliament, 2
Agencies, 5
Arbitration, 52
Associated employers
 Definition of, 18

C

Closed shop, 51
Codes of practice, 34
COHSE, 50–51
Collective bargaining, 49, 51
Commission for Racial Equality, 34
Common law, 2
Confidentiality, 9
 Professional responsibility and, 9
Constructive dismissal, 14, 24
Continuous employment
 Definition of, 17
Contract of employment, 6
 Changes in, 13
 Express terms, 11
 Form of, 7
 Implied terms, 8
 Right to written statement of, 7

D

Damages, 6, 16
 Unfair dismissal, 29
Employed status, 3
Differentials
 Justifications for, 36
Direct discrimination, 32
Discrimicantion
 Remedies for, 34
Discrimination, indirect, 32
Dismissal
 Allowed reasons for, 25
 Definition of, 24
 Trade union-related, 51
Duties
 Refusal to perform, 53
Duty of care, 6

E

EC law, 2, 31
Employees with split responsibilities, 46
Employees' obligations, 9–10
Employers' duties, 9
Employers' rules, 14
Employment Appeal Tribunal, 23
Employment contract
 NHS, 42
Employment contracts
 Equality clause, 35
Employment Protection (Consolidation) Act, 7
Employment status, 2
Equal Opportunities Commission, 34
Equal pay, 2, 35
Equal Pay Act, 7, 31, 35
Equal work
 Definition of, 35
Ethnic group
 Definition of, 33
European Community law, 3–4

F

Fellow workers
 Employers' duties, 9
Fixed-term contracts
 Ending of, 15
 Premature termination of, 16
Fringe benefits, 12

G

Gross misconduct, 16

H

Holidays, 12
Hours of work, 12

I

Illegal employment
   Dismissal, 27
Implied terms, 6
Incompetence
   Dismissal in relation to, 25
Industrial action, 52–54
Industrial tribunals, 23, 28, 34
Insurance, 6

J

Job description, 11

L

Labour Party
   Trade union affiliation to, 49
Letter of appointment, 7
Loyalty
   Employer's right to, 9

M

Maternity, 37
Maternity leave, 38–39
Maternity pay, 2
   Statutory, 37
Maternity Scheme
   Whitley, 39
Misconduct
   Dismissal and, 26
   Industrial, 26
   Non-work related, 26
   Professional, 26
Mobility clause, 20

N

National Health Service, 41
   See also NHS
National Health Service etc. Act 1990, 45
National Insurance, 38
NHS disciplinary procedure, 42
NHS disciplnary procedure, 41
NHS grievance procedure, 41
NHS negotiating bodies, 41
NHS pay bargaining, 41
NHS Rules, 1
NHS Trusts, 1, 45
Notice periods, 17
NUPE, 50–51

O

Overtime bans, 53

P

Pay rates, 11
Pay review body, 41, 51
Pension schemes
   Occupational, 37
Pensions
   Sexual discrimination and, 37
Pink, Nurse Graham, 10
Place of employment, 11

Q

Qualifications
   Lack of, 26

R

Race Relations Act, 31
   Exceptions to, 33
Racial discrimination, 31, 33
Recruitment
   Discrimination in, 32
Redundancies
   Trade unions' right of consultation, 20
Redundancy, 2

Alternative employment and, 20
Definition of, 19
Selection for, 20
Statutory scheme, 19
Unfair dismissal and, 27
Redundancy payments, 21
Religious discrimination, 33
Relocation, 20
Restructuring
 Redundancy and, 21
Retainer schemes, 39
Retirement age, 37
 Unfair dismissal in relation to, 24
Royal College of Nursing, 50

S

Self-employment, 1
Sex discrimination, 2
Sex Discrimination Act, 31
Sexual discrimination, 31, 34
Sexual harassment, 9, 34
Sickness
 Fixed-term contracts and, 15
 Long-term, 25
 Repeated minor, 26
SMP
 See Maternity pay, statutory
SSP
 See Statutory Sick Pay
Statutes, 2
Statutory entitlements, 3
Statutory Sick Pay, 2
Strikes, 53

T

Termination of employment, 14
Trade Union Membership, 50
Trade union reform, 49
Trade Unions, 49
 Membership responsibilities, 51
 Nature of, 49
 Political funds, 50
Treaty of Rome, 3, 35

U

UKCC, 1
UKCC Rules, 10
Unemployment benefit, 2
Unfair dismissal, 2, 23
 Burden of proof, 24
 Definition of, 23
 Entitlement to claim for, 24
 Industrial action and, 54
 Remedies for, 29
United Kingdom Central Council
 See UKCC

W

Whistle blowers, 41
Whistle-blowing, 10, 12
Whitley Council, 1, 41
Whitley Maternity Scheme, 39
Work to grade, 10
Work to rule, 10
Working to grade, 54
Wrongful dismissal
 Definition of, 23